BORN AGAIN

THE WARRIORS OF CANCER

AF657986

MEENA JHA
DR. SHRUTI JHA

Clever Fox®
PUBLISHING
Chennai • Bangalore

CLEVER FOX PUBLISHING
Chennai, India

Published by CLEVER FOX PUBLISHING 2025
Copyright © Meena Jha 2025

All Rights Reserved.
ISBN: 978-93-7500-101-0

This book has been published with all reasonable efforts taken to make the material error-free after the consent of the author. No part of this book shall be used, reproduced in any manner whatsoever without written permission from the author, except in the case of brief quotations embodied in critical articles and reviews.

The Author of this book is solely responsible and liable for its content including but not limited to the views, representations, descriptions, statements, information, opinions and references ["Content"]. The Content of this book shall not constitute or be construed or deemed to reflect the opinion or expression of the Publisher or Editor. Neither the Publisher nor Editor endorse or approve the Content of this book or guarantee the reliability, accuracy or completeness of the Content published herein and do not make any representations or warranties of any kind, express or implied, including but not limited to the implied warranties of merchantability, fitness for a particular purpose. The Publisher and Editor shall not be liable whatsoever for any errors, omissions, whether such errors or omissions result from negligence, accident, or any other cause or claims for loss or damages of any kind, including without limitation, indirect or consequential loss or damage arising out of use, inability to use, or about the reliability, accuracy or sufficiency of the information contained in this book.

A PRAYER TO MY LORD SHREE SAI RAM

Lord Sai I am writing a book on my own suffering which I went through while battling Cancer. You were a part of my journey so you know it all. You were by my side due to which I could endure such a big fight and come out healthy. This book is the tale of all those people who have ever suffered with the disease. I am one of the lucky few who came out of it and today I am sitting here to write this book. When I recite my story let my eyes not mist or my pen not falter in its expression. With your grace let the story be a motivator for all those suffering in pain. Let the hope of being out of pain and suffering become their strength and let them alight a new path to health and happiness in which they become a hope for others.

Lord Sai Ram, Param Brahma Bhagwan you reside inside all human beings and whenever I have to feel your presence I just need to close my eyes and feel your light in me; like the spirit of truth and perseverance. Please hold my hand just the way you have always held the hand of all your disciples. Bless me the way you graced Annasaheb when he was writing Sai Satcharitra. Bless my pen with your piousness so that it flows with the richness of language and provides all my readers the strength and blesses them to move to the path of recovery.

Om Sai Ram. May peace reign in the hearts of all our readers.

CONTENTS

ACKNOWLEDGEMENT

This book is my reflection of truth, suffering and revival. I would like to give a special thanks to Aditya Nath Jha, who believed I can show my perspective to the world and it was he who wanted me to write this book for those who are fighting Cancer. My two little girls Shruti and Shreya who silently prayed for my recovery and were my motivation to bear the mindless pain. My mother and father, they prayed mindlessly and went temple to temple praying for my good health. I do not remember my childhood but at the age of 39 my mother held my hand and helped me to walk again. Mummy and Papa I am really sorry for putting you through this pain but I think it was destiny we were all fated for it.

One of the major motivations to look beyond pain came from the medical fraternity from the head of Muljibhai hospital Dr. Mahesh Desai, my oncologist and urologist Dr. Shashi Kant Mishra and his better half Dr. Vandana Mishra, who are currently running Precision Hospital at Lucknow. The way they look at pain and their commitment towards humanity need to be acknowledged. Dr. Shashi Kant Mishra handled my case brilliantly. It has taught me big lessons in empathy and resilience. I would like to thank Ms. Ami Shah who taught me Reiki and helped me overcome the lasting pain which chemotherapy had left inside me. Deepti Ghatge who shared her experience about mindfulness and the way of meditation. I would like to thank

Matthew George Chandy, Gopal Sham Krishnan and Michelle from Karunasharaya hospice at Bangalore for sharing their invaluable experience with me.

I would like to thank all my family members and my Reiki friends who were there all the time praying for my good health. I would like to acknowledge my special thanks to all those people who shared their story of pain recovery with us. They are warriors who conquered the disease with iron intent. Many patients who wanted to keep their identity a secret their names have been changed.

ABOUT THE AUTHOR

The book is written by Ms. Meena Jha and Dr. Shruti Jha. Meena Jha is a Cancer Warrior herself. She fought a bitter battle of pain back to health which made a deep impact in her mind. Her daughter Dr. Shruti Jha was then just 11 years old and had seen her mother battle the disease. Meena Jha's health depletion made Shruti resolute to take up medicine as a profession at a later date in life.

Meena Jha is an MBA Finance who worked for various financial institutions where she headed the corporate training division for them. She currently trains, writes, authors books and writes blogs, to teach and engage with young minds in schools and colleges.

Dr. Shruti Jha is a qualified medical doctor and an ICMR STS scholar. She has published research papers in renowned journals namely in Journal of Postgraduate Medical Education and Research of PGIMER, Chandigarh, Indian Journal of Health Sciences and Biomedical Research (KLEU), National Journal of Medical Research, and SBV Journal of Basic Clinical and Applied Health Science.

The emotional journey of cancer of her mother as a cancer survivor inspired her to take up the field of Medicine and made her deeply interested to co-author with her in the process of writing the book. She has keen interest in the field of public health, research methodology, radiology and oncology.

PREFACE

Cancer is a word which people fear to talk about and discuss due to the catastrophic effect it has on people's lives. Many of us do not realise when we become critically ill and it is after thorough examination by the specialists people get to know they are affected by a deadly disease. Though science has developed and there are many kinds of therapies, medicines and advanced methodology of surgery available for the treatment of the disease, however, the journey to wellness is extremely painful. It needs the careful and understanding attention of a caregiver both at home and at the hospital.

While getting treated for urinary bladder cancer I realised the kind of doctors I was getting the attention, were no ordinary people. The amount of empathy and compassion they showed to each patient was much beyond my imagination. They could understand the fact that most of us were reeling under the shock and fear of being affected by the disease. The patients looked at the doctors with hope in their eyes, to get respite and get a second chance to live.

Most oncologists are professionals by their attitude which is part of their work ethos. They also show a lot of human understanding towards the patient and their families. While the patient is fearful for their own life, the family members are also under trauma, they need an equal amount of understanding and their concerns need to be heard and addressed along with the patient. The fear of losing a near and dear one is immense. Most of the doctors are calm by nature and are usually good at counselling sessions. The meeting with the doctors finds peace with the ill patients and the mentally grieving family. A medical practitioner needs to be emotionally resilient to work under such emotional and mental pressure. On an everyday basis the problem-solving and diagnostic skills of a doctor are put to test. They are aware of the expectation of the patients and their families which is tough for professionals to fulfil all the time. They are aware of the limitations of being a doctor and the medical practice, however it is tough to explain to people many times.

It has been 13 years ever since I was treated for Urinary Bladder Cancer. I tried forgetting the whole incident but it was a futile exercise. It never did erase from my mind. The pain I went through has faded but the impact in my mind was so severe that I think I will remember it till the day I die. I look at it as a journey in which I was never alone. Along with me was a young doctor couple Dr. Shashikant Mishra and Dr. Vandana Mishra toiling mindlessly to get me out of the pain and disease. The entire process of my treatment went on for more than a year where on and off I was called to the hospital for surgery and consultation.

During the period I was also aware of the turmoil which the doctors were going through in their personal life. They did not have leisure to discuss their pain in public nor express their personal grief. They would just put it aside with a smile and get back to the agenda of wellness of the patient. The doctor couple treating me were quite young and the way they treated their personal loss gave me strength to stand up to the situation and fight for my life and make the necessary changes which I needed to. I decided to wipe the tears of my emotionally worn out mother and be by the side of my agonised children and husband.

The sole reason for writing this book is to show the emotional, psychological and medical journey of a patient and a doctor when they fight this deadly disease as a team. It is a beautiful teamwork of spirit and belief which the duo share among themselves which makes a winning team. I am of the firm belief, your medicines will affect you best when you take it with the belief that it will provide you health and this needs a healthy mind to think clearly. From the last thirteen years I have not taken any medicine without consulting my oncologist and the faith that I share with him has never failed me. This book is about some survivors and their eminent oncologists who have given their entire life treating people, their personal journey, achievements, personal griefs and the accolades they achieved in their way of life.

This book is an appreciation and tribute to the spirit shown by these warring doctors and patients who win because of their winning mindset and the mutual sense of respect for each other. My book is for those in pain and the doctors treating the ailing who need to become a source of hope for the people they treat and for those patients who need to learn to respect the medical fraternity and believe in them while getting treated. Through this book I would like to cherish the memory of those ingenious specialists who have given their entire life to bring people out of pain. The spirit of those family members needs to be remembered with loads of love as they stand by their people in pain and despair.

I hope this book reaches the hearts of millions so that they can treat grieving people with love, affection and understanding when they are sick and ailing.

Meena Jha

UNDERSTANDING CANCER: THROUGH A DOCTORS EYES

Cancer, as a disease, is a rollercoaster of emotions, an ordeal of the last birth considered by few, or maybe some think it to be a curse. In reality, it doesn't look the way it is perceived by most people. On the contrary, it is like any other disease that needs to be screened and diagnosed at an early stage. The constant taboos and the representation of this disease is deadly, due to the lack of awareness, have resulted in innocent people losing their lives because the disease reaches an advanced stage due to a lack of understanding about undergoing screening at the right time. Let us understand in detail, debunk some myths about cancer, and understand why cancer is still so difficult to treat.

Debunking the myths

When we hear the word cancer, then there is a sense of hysteria, which is because of multiple myths, like in earlier times, when most of the cancer patients were treated by native medicine or taken to religious places, as it was considered either a possession by demons or some curse by God. It's with the development of modern science that it was proved that cancer is a disease that requires medical attention and treatment.

Many assume that all lumps and moles are cancerous, but many of them are benign, like they normally exist without affecting the body; only when you feel pain or see an increase in size requires medical attention. Basically every lump in the breast or abnormal growth is not cancerous, but bringing it to the attention of a doctor is still necessary for ascertaining whether it is benign or malignant. A biopsy is the cornerstone of cancer diagnosis, which is necessary for diagnosis and treatment purposes.

Cancer can happen to anyone irrespective of the person's lifestyle because there are multiple factors involved for a person to develop cancer, like genetic or family history. The disease is a threat not just to people who drink, smoke, or have a unhealthy lifestyle. There is a risk factor for all of us to develop cancer.

With the development of technology and minimally invasive methods, cancer treatment is becoming less painful, and better treatment outcomes and survival rates have been achieved recently. The treatment and the longevity of life of a cancer patient depends on the staging of the cancer and how the patient responds to the treatment, which determines the treatment outcome and survival rates.

Your healthcare provider, who advises you for radiotherapy or chemotherapy, also explains all the possible adverse effects before starting the treatment. A lot of prerequisites are taken into consideration during chemotherapy.

Constant hydration, rest, and a peaceful environment at home are needed when patients are undergoing chemotherapy. A test dose is given to the patient before checking for adverse effects. If the patient does not develop any adverse effects, then the treatment is continued. Constant rest, hydration, and nutrition are necessary along with chemotherapy to make it less painful.

Pollution is another factor that is mentioned as a reason for developing cancer. There are many other factors, like the carcinogenicity level and duration of exposure; also, it needs to be kept in mind that it is less dangerous than smoking and tobacco use.

Not all kinds of cancer affect a patient's fertility. Cancer that affects the reproductive organs only affects the fertility of the patients, but there are multiple options if fertility needs to be preserved before the cancer treatment, like freezing of eggs or storing of semen.

It is always necessary to see a doctor at any stage of diagnosis. An annual screening is always advisable, as prevention is always better than cure.

Understanding Cancer

Let's take a deep breath, close our eyes, and see what exactly this disease is all about. Let's imagine that there is a patient for whom a very small amount of tissue has been taken for histopathological examination to confirm the diagnosis of cancer. The tissue is taken, slides are prepared, and observed under a microscope. To your surprise, you search the slide and see a sea filled with water, and your cells are the sand on the beach. Then suddenly, you see the burrowing of a creature, and when you look closely, you spot a crab. In the human body, the cancer cells appear to be like the body and legs of a crab. Ladies and gentlemen, boys and girls, you have found the little imposter : "the notorious cancer."

History of Cancer

My dear readers, by standing near the beach, you identified the imposter named Cancer. A wise man has always said that before winning over an enemy, you should gather complete information about the strengths and weaknesses of your opponent as a secret sauce to success. Let's now take a deep dive into the word cancer. Let me ask you a question: Who is the father of medicine? Yes, you have guessed it correctly; it is 'Hippocrates.' In his era, when he saw malignant cells with swollen veins, there was limited technology. So, when he observed tumors with swollen veins, he named it karkinos in Greek, which was later coined as cancer in Latin, adopted by Roman physicians. All these words mean the same thing: a crab. The imposter was identified at the macroscopic level in advanced stages at a later date. This was due to the absence of a device that is so accessible today, which allows you to see things more clearly and identify the smallest details.

Yes, my dear friends, I am talking to you about Antonie van Leeuwenhoek's gift to mankind: 'the microscope.' However, the question arises as to how we still identify cancer under a microscope. There are some notable people; Ibn Sina, also known as Avicenna, documented the local spread of cancer based on how the disease develops in a breast cancer patient, as mentioned in the Canon of Medicine.

Edwin Smith Papyrus was the first to describe cancer, including cancers of the uterus, stomach, and skin. Jean Claude Recamier was the one to coin the term metastasis, which means to migrate in Greek. This explains why cancer in one area has the potential to spread to multiple places, just like a nomad making a home in various locations within a caravan, as explained by Stephen Paget based on his seed and soil hypothesis. The seed is the cancer cell, and the soil is the organ with which it is in close contact.

The question arises: how is secondary metastasis possible in the environment? Seed dispersal occurs through air, water, insects, or animals in plants. Similarly, if an area that is in direct communication with these cancer cells interacts with nearby organ cells, blood vessels, and lymph nodes, the cancer will spread to nearby organs and, over time, to distant organs as well. Theodor Boveri was the one who stated that cancer can be caused by mutations. Percivall Pott was the one who identified the first etiology of cancer, discovering that chimney sweepers developed scrotum cancer due to increased risk from soot. This was the foundation of oncology. B.J. Kennedy, recognized as the father of oncology globally, and Dr. Suresh H. Advani, known in India, have made notable contributions to the understanding of multiple myeloma, leukemia treatment, and hematopoietic stem cell transplantation, respectively.

The Clinical Check

In a nutshell, cancer can be described as the complex syndrome (group of diseases) that is characterised by uncontrolled abnormal proliferation of cells. It can either spread locally, or it can spread through distant sites through blood or lymph nodes. The causes of cancer can be through direct exposure to the environment, like constant sunlight exposure and lack of melanin for skin cancer. Constant exposure to soot for chimney sweepers, high exposure to red meat, health conditions that might reduce our immunity like obesity, diabetes, hypertension, HIV, TB, patients with organ transplantation, lifestyle changes like substance abuse, alcohol, smoking, and nicotine use like betel nut chewing, etc.

Patients develop difficulty in breathing, uncontrolled diarrhoea or constipation, uncontrolled growth, and pain on the site; they may also develop a fever and may develop bleeding from any site depending on the site. They might experience fatigue, weakness, and loss of appetite; experience pain during micturition; have abdominal pain, swelling in any part of the body, and get swollen lymph nodes.

Excision and biopsy, PET, CECT, and MRI; clinical examination; and laboratory investigation for the tumour markers and histopathological examination or fine needle aspiration cytology of that area are used for diagnosis other than a very comprehensive history and exhaustive clinical examination in order to stage the disease.

Does our body actually communicate with us?

The million-dollar question is when someone who intends to do harm enters our body, then how come our body does not do anything? The answer to this question is a dialogue of Shah Rukh Khan from Chennai Express, which is to never underestimate the power of a common man. At the time of danger, it is the common man who fights against all odds. The same goes with our body as well. There is a very strong and robust force inside us that has fought against multiple diseases, which is none other than our immune system. Normally, when cell injury happens, then inflammatory markers and tumour suppressor genes fight against the irritant and destroy the agent and engulf it. Cancer can happen only when there is repeated irreversible cell damage beyond a point that the immune system is not able to tackle. For example, any etiological agent that is causing cell injury on the outside, like the repeated sun exposure without sunscreen, will cause cell injury, which will cause the mutation of melanocytes; melanin and reactive oxygen species will lead to DNA damage and the release of which will lead to the abnormal growth of melanocytes, mostly in the development of small moles, which, with years, would develop into a large mole and then later might turn into melanoma.

In a similar way, the body does communicate with us when it is in pain; it depends on us to be kind enough to listen to the cries of our own body. This stage is known as the precancerous stage, where the body will show all the symptoms. Like uncontrolled bleeding from any part of the body, presence of a swelling, any long-standing benign conditions like inflammatory bowel disease, peptic ulcer disease, Barrett's oesophagus, uncontrolled constipation or diarrhoea, and any long-standing pain in any part of the body. If you develop any long-standing disease that is affecting the activity of daily life, it should be immediately reported to a doctor.

Last Question

The last question that might be there in your mind is the fact that the treatment of cancer is approached so differently even after so many technological advancements. I will analyse this differently as to why there are gaps in awareness about cancer treatment in people. I will answer this question in a comprehensive manner with a PESTEL analysis. The topic will be approached from all perspectives, i.e., political, economical, social, technological, environmental, and legal.

Political Factor

According to the National Cancer Act of 1971 of the USA, which was signed by President Nixon to expand and coordinate the national effort against cancer. India, under the National Programme for Prevention and Control of Cancer, Diabetes, Cardiovascular Diseases, and Stroke, the government spends a considerable budget on cancer screening and even works in collaboration with private hospitals to run awareness camps, but the pain and the hysteria associated with cancer are so strong that people are unwilling to come forward for screening. Many people who are even diagnosed with the disease are often scared of the cost that is incurred and the debts that the family would undergo through the treatment process. Many patients who are from poor backgrounds have a higher possibility of availing themselves of treatment available under the govt. Schemes. The question arises are those hospitals amply equipped to handle Cancer patients? It is very important to create strong policies and educate people so that they can create stronger initiatives to promote education about cancer, simple methods to examine cancer on their own, and the importance of timely screening especially if there is a history of cancer in the family.

Economic factors

People from lower and lower middle class backgrounds don't take initiative in cancer screening programs, namely yearly body checkups, because of the cost that is incurred or the fear of losing a day's payment especially for the labour classes. Most importantly, the fear of losing the job due to leaves in the process of treatment or the fear of family debts that might accumulate during the cancer treatment process.

Speaking about the different Government schemes, there are schemes like the Health Minister's Cancer Patient Fund (HMCPF), which provides coverage up to 2 lakhs for poor patients or 5 lakhs in emergency cases. The Health Minister's Discretionary Grants (HMDG), which provides assistance up to Rs.50,000 to poor patients; and the Central Government Health Scheme (CGHS) for the retired central government employees. The National Health Protection Scheme and the Pradhan Mantri Jan Arogya Yojana provides Rs. 5,000 per year per family in secondary and tertiary hospitalisation. Rashtriya Arogya Nidhi provides Rs 5 lakhs towards the treatment. The Prime Minister's National Relief Fund provides partial coverage for cancer treatment, heart surgeries, liver transplants, and organ transplants. There is also a State Illness Assistance Fund, which is set up by all states and union territories.

The Chief Minister's Free Cancer Chemotherapy Scheme provides chemotherapy drugs to 1000 patients per year at concessional rates. Pradhan Mantri Bhartiya Janaushadhi Pariyojana is for affordable drugs. Affordable Medicines and Reliable Implants for Treatment (AMRIT) Pharmacy stores provide cancer drugs at discounted prices. The main reason I am mentioning these schemes is that there is a lack of awareness about such schemes, leading to debts in the family of the patients. There needs to be an awareness regarding these government programs so that cancer treatment is accessible to all those who need it.

Social factors

People who suffer from cancer often face a lot of social issues from their families; particularly if it has occurred to a woman. They are often forced to face social neglect or are at times also abandoned. Families who are taking care of such patients should be aware of these concessions that can be availed of by the patient. All cancer patients who are undergoing any cancer treatment get a benefit of a 50 percent concession in plane fare by Air India from their hometown to the treatment centre. In train travel, 100% concession in AC 3 tier or sleeper class, 75% on AC second class and 50% concession on AC chair car. The patient should produce a certificate when applying for the scheme from the institute or the hospital where the patient is undergoing treatment. The doctor, nurse, and pharmacists are the first points of contact for these patients. They should take the initiative in helping the patients to avail financial support because most of the time these are the stumbling blocks in cancer treatment.

Technological factors

The most advanced treatment, providing painless, minimally invasive, and better prognosis treatment, is still very expensive, or they are perceived to be very expensive. The institutes of national importance of our country, notably AIIMS New Delhi, JIPMER, PGIMER Chandigarh, and NIMHANS, and many well known medical colleges have the expertise to tackle these cases in all the states of the country and are always willing to support the patients care at affordable rates. Still the patients are not willing to undergo the investigation because of various myths and taboos or fear attached to it. India is a very price-sensitive country, and people still tend to have a disbelief in the medical system even if the facility of CT scan or MRI is made available to them at affordable rates. In many situations, people are reluctant to get treated in government set-ups due to lack of faith in the system.

Environmental factors

The government and public should share the challenge of fighting cancer as a shared responsibility. The issue of rising pollution of air, water, and land is a risk factor, and chronic exposure is a health risk that can lead to the rise in the number of cases of cancer. Students in schools and colleges should take even more interest in spreading awareness about cancer prevention, diagnosis, and treatment. All of us, as responsible citizens of the country, should understand that a healthy planet means a healthy country, which means our health is our top priority. A healthy community is the foundation of an industrious country.

Legal factors

A strong surveillance system should be developed, and all the high-risk groups for cancer should be intensively screened, and vaccinations for cervical cancer should be made mandatory for high-risk groups. It should be made mandatory to create awareness about health days, and necessary screening should be made mandatory for such patients. The health care services and patient rights should be made aware to everyone, and private institutions should take initiatives in creating awareness about spreading information, which is not being done stringently in our country.

Conclusion

Our laid back approach is the reason that our country is struggling in the implementation of the government led initiatives. It is due to this that we have gaps in the awareness about cancer and its treatment. Spreading the awareness is not just the responsibility of the government but also the citizens, namely a doctor, nurses, pharmacists, and each and every citizen should take it up as a shared responsibility. What you see is what you perceive, just like when you see the word IMPOSSIBLE, it says I'M POSSIBLE. When we work towards our goal with full zeal and fervour, that is the day when you would find that the entire universe is conspiring to make it possible. Even your fight against cancer is possible.

THE STORY OF DR. MAHESH DESAI

This is the story of Dr. Mahesh Ramanlal Desai. Who took his fathers words to his heart and decided to become a medical professional but with a difference. As he relates his story to me today I find the tears shimmering in his eyes. At the age of 82 even today the scar of his mothers death is as alive as it was when he was the age of 17. He relives that painful moment while he remembers the tragic incident from his childhood.

A boy around the age of 17 was sitting outside the operation theatre. He knew from the people around him and the elders who spoke in hushed tones that his mother had been bleeding profusely and a very senior doctor had prescribed surgery which needed to be performed immediately. They said that she was suffering from excessive uterine bleeding. He was too small to decode the medical jargon. The only thing he knew was his mother was bleeding heavily and she needed medical attention.

The teenager prayed to God for his mother's recovery along with his three other siblings. He was the youngest amongst the four and his parents loved him very fondly. He was a quiet and serious boy, he loved his books and studied hard at school. He had always been a good boy and obeyed his parents. He prayed hard to all the deities of the world to keep his mother in good health so that he could take her back home and take care of her.

Mr. Ramanlal Desai walked through the corridor all tensed and worked up. Dhanlaxmiben, his wife, had always possessed good health and was an active person. She had raised her four children with loads of love and affection. She had worked tirelessly for the health and the financial wealth of her family. Today all her loved ones were sitting outside the OT room with a worry on their face and a prayer in their heart.

The senior doctor came out of the operation theatre looking worried and sorrowful. He patted the arm of Mr Desai and said something which was audible to people around him. Mr. Desai stood rooted to the spot for a while and could not move for a long time before he broke down sobbing on a nearby chair. The teeny boy named Mahesh shivered at the reaction of his father and came to the doctor. As a matter of fact all his siblings and relatives were surrounding the Doctor now. He looked at them and said, "Sorry". A one syllable word which made a crashing and deafening noise.

The little boy found the shaky voice in his throat and asked him, "How is my mother?" The doctor looked at him and explained that she was no more, he said, "It was a one in a million complication in my hand", and the doctor left the family to mourn for their loss. Little Mahesh could not understand much of what was told to him. He just knew that he had lost the most loving person on the face of this earth. The maternal hand which patted his head was no more and there would be no more cosy midnight chats with her and he had lost someone who whipped his most favourite food for him. He moaned and cried as he had never done in his life.

His father had assured him before the procedure that his mother who had been sick for a long time would come back hale and hearty very soon. Life would be back to normal and the family would get back to its blissful state as before. Poor Mahesh went and sat by his father whose body racked with sobs. His father knew about his affection for his mother and the loss and hollowness the little boy must be going through inside him. His father held him and cried. He spoke between his sobs and told his little son that he needs to be a doctor in future and see to it that families do not suffer at the loss of their loved ones. The pain little Mahesh went through became his strength later in life to become a famous surgeon and urologist.

Dr.Mahesh Ramanlal Desai today is the founder member of the Muljibhai Hospital. A surgeon by profession he stays busy with his patients who are lined up for his attention and professional care. People all across India and abroad come to him for his medical advice and take the advantage of fine skills of surgery for different kinds of urological diseases.

The reason I am with him today is because he is not only a fine doctor and an authority in his field. He too battled the disease of Cancer. Being a Cancer survivor myself I know the immense pain people go through while battling the disease. I wanted to know a doctor's journey and the perspective of the disease. I remember meeting him before my surgery and his reassurance in which he told me that his team of Oncologists were masters in their work and I would be out of danger without any trouble. These surgeons were his students and he had full confidence in his team.

True to his word I was operated on by one of the best surgeons in his team Dr. Shashikant Mishra, a young Urologist and Oncologist by profession, assured me of getting me back to good health soon.

It has been thirteen years of my treatment. After writing my first book on mental wellness of people. I decided to take a personal journey inward and tried reconciling my thoughts about one of the most dreaded diseases. The journey with this disease is like being burnt in hell. I had decided never to think and talk about it ever in my life. However, I changed my mind and decided to meet up again with Dr. Desai and exchange my thoughts with him and ask about his welfare.

Rendezvous With Dr. Mahesh Desai

Meeting Dr. Desai is not easy. Even at his age he keeps himself busy with his patients and his OPD lobby is always full. As I enter the OPD which leads to his consultation room. I can see the faces of anxious people waiting to meet the doctor regarding the health of their loved ones. My mind throws back to those days when I used to visit Dr. Mishra with my husband and my 4 year old daughter. Before entering the place I would go and visit the temple of Lord Sainath and seek his blessings so that the investigation and meeting with the doctor goes well.

I have been waiting for three hours now and I have not been able to meet Dr. Desai as he is in a serious operation battling for the life of a one year old child. I spoke to his secretary Mr. Jose and postponed the meeting for the next day at 8 in the morning. A time when the doctor is relatively free and I can speak to him at length.

After ten years I had the good opportunity to meet Dr. Desai in his cabin. I was accompanied by my husband. I needed the strength of my better half to walk through the lobby. The pain and uncertainty of the yesteryears came flooding back into my mind.

As I opened the door I saw a man whom I did not recognise. I remember a smiling stout doctor reassuring me when I had met him last. He looked fit and his health shone through his eyes.

Me and my husband sat down after my initial introduction, he enquired me about my health. I told the doctor that my reason for meeting him is to capture his personal journey as a cancer patient and his life ever since. His journey as a doctor and the reasons why at his age he still finds the energy to come back and combat such deadly disease.

Dr. Desai is a senior surgeon and a complete institution in himself. After completing his MS from India he went ahead and did his FRCS from London. He is usually serious and loves to speak at length. He went ahead and related the story of his mothers death and then said that there are many lives attached to that one person who is sick. When you give treatment and health to a sick person, you are actually giving health and happiness to the entire family. If the Doctor could have put my mother back to health on that fateful day, the life of my family would have been different. I see the face of my mother every time I treat a sick person.

As an onlooker I could see the little Mahesh still sitting by his mothers side grieving her death. I could understand his feelings as my own daughter was just eleven years old during my illness. Her fear, anxiety and pain was something I had seen and felt on my nerves. My eyes misted seeing his grief.

As the conversation went ahead I moved onto capturing his story as a patient.

Dr. Desai, how did you get to know you were suffering from cancer?

It was during a checkup one day I noticed that I saw a growth on my kidney and thought it was a small cyst. Then I saw a further growth in its size and I knew it was a tumour. After further investigation it was found to be cancerous growth. I knew better than anyone I will have to get it operated on.

What did you do then?

I knew I would have to get it operated on as early as possible.

Who was your doctor?

My son Dr. Mihir Desai, who is a surgeon and settled in the USA, was my surgeon. He is trained in Robotic surgery and he performed the procedure.

At what stage was the Cancer detected?

It was at a very beginning stage. The tumour was very small.

Did you go through chemotherapy and any other kind of treatment?

I did not have to go through any chemotherapy or radio therapy as the growth was extremely small.

How long did it take for you to get back to work?

I was back to work after five days of rest.

Doctor people take years to come out of this disease, just five days and then back to work. That is miraculous.

People usually do not understand the fact that this disease can occur in any body and it needs to be detected and treated as any other disease. Our body is like any other mechanical device which needs to be checked and treated for optimal functionality. Look at it from the scientific perspective things will be simpler to understand.

Doctor, do you see yourself retiring in a few years?

I would not like to retire ever in my lifetime. I would like to lead my life attending my patients till the day I die. I find peace with my work.

Doctor, do you believe in Karma? Many people told me that such a deadly disease is the result of your past life karma. Do you believe in it?

Okay, I will come back to science again and then to Karma. When a sperm and an Ova fertilise a zygote is formed. The zygote goes through a process of mutation of cells and then a body is developed. This is life. Sometimes this process of mutation goes out of control in some parts of the body for many reasons. Then a cancerous growth takes place. This can be due to bad eating habits, excessive smoking or drinking, there is a lot of preservative in food, excessive use of fertiliser in food etc. The list is endless.

Now coming back to Karma. As a human being I have no idea how people account for their Karma. So I would not comment about it. I am a strong believer in God and I know there is a superior power above us who guides us. I believe in him and lead my life.

What changes did you make to your lifestyle and daily routine?

Morning for about 1 ½ hours I do exercise and then go to the hospital at 7.30 am. Coming back home depends upon the work at around 6 or 7 p.m. Then I do my research studies in the late evening. Earlier I used to go back home at around 10.30 p.m. I follow a lovely ayurvedic diet. It helps me to detox and keep healthy.

What are some early symptoms which people should watch out for?

Do regular check up, early detection. Early cancer does not have any symptoms.

If there is one perception which you would like to change about the perception of the disease, what would it be?

When a person is born and he starts growing there is always the possibility of diseases like polio,flu, infectious diseases etc. Anyone can get infected by any disease.

At the age of 82, people look up to you for life. You are a doctor, a surgeon, a guide, a mentor and a teacher. What are your future plans? How do you think people like us can be of use to you?

I think 3 things to be kept in mind for good health. Exercise, healthy food, avoid smoking, tobacco, excessive alcohol and if you have a family history of diabetes, blood pressure, prostate cancer, breast cancer follow up check up is needed.

People like you can do it by spreading the word around for regular check up help doctors to conduct camps and donation for poor patients. We as doctors do a lot of surgeries for free. I will be conducting camps and screen young children for diseases and provide them with the needed medication and surgery if required. I believe that people should have a good quality life which should not get compromised due to an untreated disease.

Dr. Desai, what would you like to communicate to the people at large and to the new budding doctors who will treat future patients.

Keep good health, exercise regularly, eat balanced food, go for regular check ups and encourage regular check ups for your patients.

A few lines to the caregivers while treating people in pain.

Medicines and reassurance to the people going through the process of recovery and trying to analyse the root cause of the disease. Always remember you can be on either side a doctor or patient. Even after being a surgeon I too had to get operated for this disease. So when people express their pain and discomfort, be with them and their families with loads of patience. It is not easy at times but it is the call of the hour. People expect a lot out of their doctors. As a doctor it is our duty to protect the honour of the profession.

Doctor Desai it is an honour and a pleasure to have listened to your story and perspective as a doctor and a patient. Your enormous amount of strength and courage to fight against the odds of such a life threatening disease provides me the courage to lead a meaningful life. I promise not to fret and worry about the past which has gone by and lead my way towards a more fulfilling tomorrow. At your age you are still a torch bearer for patients like us and doctors who want to become promising surgeons like you. I wish you the very best in life and if there are any unfulfilled dreams, I will pray to Lord Sai Ram for its fulfilment.

A SNEAK PEAK INTO BREAST CANCER

The Ode to an evolution of Breast

In this fast-paced life, we often find peace and solace with our loved ones while imagining the lush green mountains with pristine flowing rivers. One notices a cow feeding her calf or, in the beautiful land of Australia, where a kangaroo is feeding her cute, innocent young one. The innocence in the eyes of her young ones and the ultimate bliss and joy in the mother's eyes give her the joy of becoming a mother.

The first ever origin of breast tissue started nearly 300 million years ago, where it began as a mere secretion from sweat glands, evolving into a source of nutrition and protection to the present-day specialized modification of sweat glands in humans. The gland contains fat cells, and the breast 's location in the chest region is also a feature of evolution. Animals like cows, kangaroos, and elephants have the abdominal location of the mammary gland. This explains the journey that this bundle of joy has traveled to become a vital part of being the bounty of endless joy for every female.

Deep Dive into the Anatomy of Mammary Gland

Breast is a modification of the sebaceous gland. Some of the first clear defining features for a woman reaching adolescent phase to the adult phase is the development of the breast tissue other than menstrual cycle and hair growth in axillary and pubic region. The development of the breast is governed by the four hormones namely oestrogen, progesterone, prolactin and oxytocin. The oestrogen hormone is responsible for the ductal proliferation, progesterone causes glandular proliferation, prolactin causes milk secretion throughout the pregnancy period and once the child is born and the moment child suckles the nipples of breast gives a positive feedback which releases oxytocin which causes the ejection of milk from the nipple areolar complex.

If we look at the anatomy of the breast then it is more like a pyramid where one always at the level of mammary alveolus from where the milk drains into mammary tubules to mammary ducts to mammary ampulla to lactiferous ducts where 15-20 lactiferous duct ends into a nipple which is surrounded by alveolar tissue which is hyperpigmentation of skin surrounding the nipples with the presence of Montgomery tubercle providing lubrication to the area through its secretion and prevention of dryness around the nipple area.

It is supported by skin, fat, ligament of cooper, rib, and multiple layers of muscle forming a projection in the upper outer quadrant of the breast which is the Axillary tail of Spence.

Other than the organ for nourishment and growth it also plays a crucial role in providing protection against trauma to any of the organs of vitality namely lungs and heart.

Understanding Breast Cancer

It is extremely important for us to understand breast cancer. Exactly who are the people who are at risk of developing breast cancer or the people who need screening for breast cancer so that detection starts early.

In patients with a BMI greater than 30 kg/meter square, in nulliparous women, women who conceive at the age of more than 35 years, and those with a history of alcohol use, smoking, hormone replacement therapy, and contraceptive pills for more than 10 years.

Women from developed countries, namely Ashkenazi (Eastern European) Jewish women, women with premalignant lesions, the presence of genetic predisposition in families with a known case of breast cancer, males with untreated gynecomastia, early menarche, and women with late menopause have a high risk of developing breast cancer.

Presentation

It is extremely important for us to be a detective to identify the symptoms at the earliest after understanding the risk factors. It is extremely important to understand the fact these are triggers that eventually cause breast cancer so the regular full body check ups are required to be done regularly for such patients. The diagnosis of asymptomatic patients of early stage breast cancer is often an incidental finding during health camps and check ups can be treated curatively.

When one identifies the symptoms which are present beyond the level of tolerance is the time when the majority of the patients present to the hospital with severe symptoms have breast cancer at an advanced stage where the extent is beyond the level with severe inflammation. These cases are inoperable if the patient presents in old age and requires palliative therapy more than curative therapy.

The patient present with lump in the breast which can be palpable on examination, presence of discharge from nipple, presence of ulceration, lymph nodes enlargement, presence of chest pain, coughing of blood, joint pain, bone pain, bony tenderness, presence of fluid in thoracic cavity causing pleural effusion and fluids in abdominal cavity causing ascites, tumour extending to other organs namely liver and ovaries, orange colour of skin, dimpling of skin, retraction of nipple, tethering of skin, skin nodules are the signs and symptoms of cancer which should be identified to the people. These signs and symptoms which are classically found in the breast cancer patients are the advanced features which could be seen in the patients at very advanced age at a stage where the cases become inoperable at later stages.

Investigation & Prevention

In today's scenario where the department of radio diagnosis and pathology has made the diagnosis of breast cancer easily accessible and possible for the patients and the treating clinicians to arrive at a definitive diagnosis. Most importantly community participation is required not just from the medical fraternity but also from the people of different walks of the society to come forward to not just promote cancer screening in not just the high risk group but also in the general population who have a risk of developing this disease.

It is the need of the hour that people in rural areas provide open participation where ASHA workers play a crucial role in identifying non-communicable disease in the household. If a case is suspected by health care workers and fraternity at an early stage then the help of the doctor should be sought. It is also requested of people to take active participation in health camps and full body check ups because they are accidentally found at early stages which can be treated.

At an individual level one can easily diagnose breast cancer by performing the self breast examination that can be taught to the patients during awareness talks. It is a more effective way to diagnose the cases at an early stage. It is really essential for the patients to understand that all the lumps in the breast are not necessarily malignant in nature. It could be benign but reporting the finding to the doctor becomes extremely pivotal in arriving at a diagnosis at an early stage. This should be ideally performed when the patient is either lying down on a mattress or while taking a bath. One needs to raise the hand. With the other hand they should palpate over the breast on all the four quadrants in a circular motion from the nipple areolar complex from centre to periphery.

Triple assessment is the mainstay of arriving at definitive diagnosis where radiological methods like mammogram and USG are used for the diagnosis of breast cancer in association with biopsy and detailed history taking and examination of the patients who are suspected of the disease are the crucial way of diagnosis. Apart from this the sentinel lymph nodes biopsy and Positron emissions tomography scan is for patients who have malignant breast tumour, to know whether the disease is poorly differentiated or well differentiated, the extent of the tumour, to know the involvement of one or both the breast, the number of lymph nodes involved, presence or absence of secondary lesions into other organs and body cavities leading to adhesions and treatment challenges in later ages. Other than this immunohistochemistry, testing for ER, PR and HER 2 neu receptors are tested for the biopsy specimen to stage the disease and arrive at a treatment for patients based on the results for sensitivity to the receptors leading to device a treatment plan suitable before or after the surgery by chemotherapy and radiotherapy. These investigations also play a key role in determining the course and prognosis of the treatment.

Cooperation of patients right from the time when the patient gets diagnosed with breast cancer plays a crucial role if the patient undergoes each and every investigation in a timely manner. Coming for follow up whenever the doctor advises. The patient and the family members should always understand that every investigation that the doctors perform is to arrive at a definitive diagnosis along with an accurate location, accurate staging, lymph nodal involvement, extent of metastasis, presence of differentiation is poorly or well differentiated whether the level needs to be confirmed where a doctor needs this investigation to arrive at a diagnosis. The patient needs to understand this and cooperate in undergoing the investigation without having any preconceived notions as these investigations are extremely crucial to arrive at the confirmatory diagnosis apart from the clinical examination.

Treatment

Surgery mainly involves the removal of the breast tissues. In case of advanced cases not just the area involved, the breast tissue and the lymph nodes are removed. Apart from this chemotherapy and radiotherapy needs to be done before or after the surgery. During the period of chemotherapy the patient is expected to have adequate rest along with a balanced diet. During this period the family should support the patient for adequate recovery of the patient. Apart from this, the patient should always understand that the chemotherapeutic agents cause a risk of toxicity in the patients.

The risk of drug reaction is extremely high in patients. It is duly expected for the patients to follow a balanced diet and hydration during the course of the treatment. The patient should duly understand that cancer is a type of terminal illness. A doctor can be considered as a warrior to treat the disease. The doctor aids in patient recovery of the patient's fight from cancer disease. The patient needs to be properly explained about the disease. The family should also be counselled about the disease. They should be properly guided about the course of the treatment. The patient should be involved and be a part of the decisions of the treatment at every step actively in order to reduce the misunderstanding and stress associated with this disease.

The patients should not take undue stress about the disease. The patient should be involved in self help groups or other forms of supportive measures to alleviate the stress and anxiety during the course of the treatment where patients can interact with each other and understand the journey of each other in order to alleviate the disease. Other than this patients are requested to maintain utmost transparency and trust while undergoing treatment. At the same time a patient who is absolutely clueless about the disease, often read from multiple sources, even going on multiple databases, search engines and even taking multiple second opinions. It should always be understood that every body has a different way to manifest a disease.

The same features of the disease might not be present in the same order. The doctor presents the disease in the most simplest way in such a way that the patient knows the things to reduce stress associated with the disease. It is duly expected from the patient to ask all the questions to your treating clinician and at the same time clinicians should be extremely patient in answering the queries of the patient. There would be times when there would be an exorbitant level of patient load or times when patients or their attenders would ask questions which could be trivial. However, by answering those questions at the golden hour wins the trust of the patients, reduces their dependability on other methods of alternate medicine, search engines, databases and even second opinion from the doctor other than your treating doctor does wonders.

The main point of concern in breast removal surgery is the cosmetic effect on the body of a woman leading to loss of confidence and self-esteem. There are young women who are suffering from cancer. There are procedures like minimally invasive surgeries, stereotactic radiosurgery are the procedures where the focused radiation beams are released in the concerned areas. These are some of the procedures apart from the conventional surgical procedures which are minimally invasive with minimal cosmetic disfigurement in early cases or with tumours that are present in small region

In a family where there is a history of breast cancer and the patient presents with features then surgical treatment is the main stay of treatment where there is a family history or there is presence of a large tumour. There should be an integrated approach in collaboration with other specialties where the patient can be explained about Silicone implants which can provide the same impact as real breast reducing the cosmetic effect for the women, boosting their morale and self confidence after the treatment.

Prevention

Once a patient who has undergone cancer treatment their body doesn't remain the same after the treatment. It is duly expected from the patient to avoid the stressors that could cause the disease to recur. The patient should maintain a balanced diet, stress free life, maintain a healthy life, and regularly exercise.

Avoid the consumption of processed food, active exercise like brisk walking should be a part of the schedule. The patient should come for regular follow-up to their treating physicians. In any circumstances the treating physician should always have an idea about medication for your generalised diseases that you are taking as high power antibiotics might create adverse effects for such patients due to weak immunity. Depending upon the type of silicone implant used, the patient needs to come for regular follow-up.

Now we would move into the next section where we would narrate to you two stories of brave and resilient ladies who survived the disease of breast cancer.

THE STORY OF ZEHRA KHAN

This is the story of Zehra Khan born and brought up in the posh locality of Bandra, Mumbai. As I sit down to talk outside her spa. The spa faces a beautiful waterbody. A 44 year beautiful Zehera sits down to rewind the story of her life. The bespectacled lovely looking woman recalls her childhood being in the care of her grandmother, mother and her elder brother. She has no recollections of her father. There were no pictures of him in the house to further her imagination. So she does not have any pictures in her mind of her missing him as she was just four when he left them.

The house was run according to strict rules and regulations laid down by her mom and her grandma. The house did not lack any number of domestic help. Everyone knew their bit of job and performed it according to what was expected out of them. Even after leading a life of lush luxury there was a kind of happiness which was missing in her family she recalls. The house lacked smiles and carefree laughter. Everything seemed to be suppressed under the mannerism, ethics and the codes laid down in the house. The little girl who abided by all the rules was not allowed to question; she just flowed along with time.

She was in her teens when she felt a furore rising inside her. She remembers all the trips she had gone out with her family to Khandala and the many trips abroad which seemed to be so regular and routine in structure like an exposure trip from school or college. I asked her many times to recount some happy memories of her visit which she refuses to think about. It was after her school life she started to find her feet on the ground with her friends. As I hear her talk, the first image which comes to her mind is of a little caged bird who had found her space in the sky after her class 10 and later learnt to fly, she spread her wings and then explored the universe.

She smiles and remembers all her school and college friends with whom she had a good time. She had always wanted to spend more time with them and enjoy life to the hilt. She recalls getting out of her car and stepping inside the crowded local train for the first time to go to college. Like all other local commuters she tried to get off a slow moving local with the help of her buddies, to avert accidents.

Though there were a lot of restrictions regarding the timings she needed to get back home on time. But the time she spent outside pursuing her bachelors in commerce gave her the needed independence and space she needed. Later in life her friends drifted into different walks of life taking serious jobs for themselves. It was her turn to give her life a serious thought and think like a career minded woman. She decided to go ahead and take up the family business and open her own spa and salon.

I was amazed to hear that she had done a seven year course in all kinds of beauty treatments in India and abroad.

"These many years to an art you must be really passionate about it".

She agreed and said that it was also her mothers business which she had run for so many years. She remembers opening her own spa and salon in the year 2010. A young girl of 24, who passionately wanted to pursue her love for the art of beauty, single mindedly.

However, her problems still persisted. She was not allowed to work till late like other upcoming entrepreneurs. The space she had been craving for since the time she was a child was still not given to her.

"There was something growing inside me. A protest, a resentment, a silent volcano which needed an outlet and I did not know what to do about it. While I looked calm from outside, I was on a complete boil. All this was creating an under confident me. I wanted to break free from the shackles and the chains which were holding me. After so many years of training I still felt under confident expressing myself as a beautician. I would not personally go ahead and attend to customers unless people really insisted", says Zehera.

She took a deep breath and then smiled and said." A few years went by and one day I met my life partner at a friend's residence. I was at her place for a visit and there he was. He was a common friend and I can just tell you that the attraction was instant for my husband, Hussain Khan. He was nothing like me. While I was conscious, he was outgoing. I was born and brought up in India and he was brought up in the UK and worked in the UK and the USA before coming back to India. He was a good looking young man. His family was in Mumbai and he had recently started a business in India. We exchanged numbers that day and started meeting each other often. I think we kept seeing each other for two years and then we decided to get married."

"My marriage was breaking away from the shackles of my childhood and helping me get into a relationship with a man I was deeply in love with. I have no words to express how I felt. We decided to go for a two month honeymoon to Europe and we kept dancing and partying the night through. My husband's extended family were broad minded and understood the aspiration of newlyweds. I was on pills to avoid pregnancy. After a few days of taking it I felt a heaviness and a burning sensation in my breast. I decided to visit a gynaecologist and consult them. She suggested that I go ahead and change my pill. So I changed my medication. For a few days it was alright and then the pain came back. It was then we decided to go back to India and start a treatment. I was two months married by then."

It was getting difficult for Zehra to continue with her story. I knew she was coming to the sad part of her story. Mother nature had given her a rude shock when she had just discovered the bliss of joyful living with the man she loved so much.

Marriage is a moment when a man and a woman discover the joy of being together and the real passion starts to flow between them. They discover in themselves the pleasure of being together which can be expressed without any inhibitions. How long happiness lives for anyone is a question no one can answer. I looked at her distant eyes busy in recollection. There were emotions which she was not comfortable sharing but still she went on.

"So I came back to Mumbai. I went to see my regular gynaecologist and explained to her the pain I was going through. She wanted to physically examine me and she felt a lump near my breast region. She immediately did an ultrasound of the breast. She felt a lump growing near it and suggested a PET scan as the next diagnostic test. It confirmed the malignancy of the tumour. My world came crashing to my feet. I was immediately taken to a leading Oncologist of India and he confirmed that the tumour had reached stage three and it had already reached my lymph nodes. The oncologist suggested surgery as the next move and he broke the news softly to me and my husband Hussain that the breast would be removed in the process."

She looked at me and smiled. "My freedom, my new found happiness and my renewed love for life all came to a screeching halt. After coming back I had straight away gone to my new home and visited my mother once in a while. All these new developments were hidden from her. I realised suddenly why she had been an overprotective mom right from the beginning. The jigsaw puzzle was suddenly falling into place. She had lost too much too early. She had wanted to protect whatever was left from her marriage. This news of my sickness would tear her apart. I kept my distance from her so that I would not fall in her lap crying like a little baby. "

From as much I had known Zehera in the last few weeks she was a strong woman and greatly believed in the power above and believed in the justice of the almighty. " I believe in a power which is not evident to the naked eye of humans. The power of God, the power of my Allah", says Zehera. My eyes misted at her words. I suddenly remembered my own days of surgery and illness. The only belief that pulled me through the entire episode was my "Sai Ram" who resides inside my heart and looks after my welfare.

"Very true, I said. When man fails, God picks up the string of life and makes things happen for you", I said. "So true Meena, I took out the holy Quran and I asked it the question if I should get a surgery done and when I looked for the answer and it said no. I tried it many times and the answer was still a no. Allah was telling me there were other ways of getting out of the situation. So I decided to go ahead and explore the issue"

This was quite unbelievable for me. In a life threatening situation you tend to take the advice coming from the doctors and other tangible sources. To stick to your own belief must have been a difficult situation.

"I started looking for solutions across the internet and I did not get much help. I met many Oncologists and spoke to them about non-invasive methods of treatment and it was of no use. Everyone suggested the removal of the affected part. No one could understand that I had just become a bride my entire life would get affected with this. I started doing research on non-invasive techniques of treatment. Then one day I came across Palbace tablets which are prescribed by the doctors in the US for the treatment of cancer.I immediately called up my oncologist and fixed up an appointment with him" said Zehera.

"When he looked at my research he said it is safe and is prescribed by the doctors in the US for the treatment of cancer. I was prescribed the course of treatment and I immediately started the treatment. I was leading a normal life, I changed my food habits to help in the healing process. I was advised to do a PET scan after a month of taking the medication. After the first month of treatment and the PET scan there was significant reduction in the size of the tumour. I continued the medication for the second month and at the end of the month, after the PET examination was done there was again a reduction in the size of the tumour. However at the end of the third month the size of the tumour remained unchanged. I went back to my Oncologist and he again started saying that surgery was the only path left for me, and I needed to make up my mind soon, this really upset me," said Zehera.

"My husband and my brother were getting quite worried for my life and they decided that we go to the US and meet a few Oncologists before we decide on any future course of treatment. So we decided to go and meet my husband's uncle who was staying in the US in New Jersey. His uncle was quite worried about my health and he would talk to me more often and suggested that we meet more doctors. All the doctors seemed to suggest the removal of the organ and I was not ready for it. "

"Then one day while we were sitting discussing things, my husband's uncle said that he had heard a talk show about a therapy for cancer. This was done by a cancer specialist and his treatment was called Radiosurgery. The name of the doctor is Dr. Gil Ledeman. We went on the net and did our research and found that he was from Harvard Medical School. He had many years of experience and had treated over 10,000 patients with the help of radiosurgery. He had treated all kinds of Cancer patients through this non-invasive treatment which is a painless method of treatment. He had his own clinic where he treated people. A lot of patients had benefited from it. The number of sessions required was decided by the doctor after seeing their condition and the history of the patient."

Zehera's eyes lit up with glow and happiness, "Suddenly I felt I was seeing light at the end of the tunnel and my hopes started to rise. My Allah was kind and showed me the path to gain my health back. Dr. Gil Lederman was based in New York and we were supposed to see him after fixing an appointment with him. We took the train to New York and went to his facility. It was a huge facility of around 5000 square feet and he had a huge team who attended to the patients along with him", Zehera spoke with a lot of enthusiasm in her voice.

"After taking my case history and initial examination of the affected part the doctor suggested sixteen sessions of radiotherapy for me. To identify the affected portion there were two tattoos made on my breast which would help them in administering the dose of radiation to the affected portion. I had to sign a consent form. I was informed about the risk, the benefits of the procedure and the tattoo would remain permanently on my body throughout my life", said Zehera.

The story was getting interesting and was generating a lot of hope. "So we booked an apartment in the city and decided to stay there while the treatment lasted. We were pre informed about the days of the treatment and we visited the facility for the sessions. Post the treatment there was a slight burning sensation on my breast and by applying a little lotion and cream it just seemed to ebb off. Post the treatment me and my husband were like any other normal newly weds on their honeymoon. We were ready to to explore the beautiful city of New York."

"I smiled at Zehera and looked at her face gleaming with warmth and happiness. " After the sixteen sessions we were heading back to India with the promise to conduct a PET post three months after the session," said Zehera, smiling ear to ear. " It might be hard to believe for people, we did go for a PET examination after three months the malignant tumour was gone. My body was free of the disease. "

I was amazed to hear the story and I was amazed to hear about the progress which science had made in the past years and the wondrous ways in which God blesses you and takes you out of situations. "I am now leading a normal life and I am running the salon and the spa on my own. I take all the stress which all normal business women take in their everyday life and see to it that I eat and sleep right."

Rendezvous With Zehra Khan

Zehra what changes did you bring into your life?

I take life as it comes. I do not hold any grudges against it if it does not turn out to be the way I wanted it to be. I have a good balanced meal and give myself the required number of hours of sleep and rest without a second thought.

What about your relationship with the people you love that go through a change as well during the time of your illness?

As my body evolved through the disease so did my relationship with the people whom I love. It is still changing.I think I need to speak my mind more. I am picking up the strings and I am practising to speak my mind. This is helping me to create peace around myself and with the people who are an integral part of my life. I was in love with Hussain and this disease has made our bond much stronger.His love and care for me grew many folds.

Do you think stressful life has anything to do with cancer?

Oh! Yes, we all need to find our place of comfort and mental peace with whatever means we can. People go for meditation and prayer sessions. I found peace with teachings in the Holy Quran and with my marriage. Though I still feel that I need to speak and express a little more than I am doing currently. I have started understanding all those things which upset me as a child. As an adult I am able to relate to it more than what I did before. Today I know my mother loves me from the core of her heart and I would never like her to know about my illness ever in my lifetime. It would tear her apart. With all her routines and schedules she was just trying to protect us.

Any future plans dear?

One day me and Hussain would like to have a baby and start a family. The sooner the better. It would be the best gift of Allah to us. It would complete me and my family.

Zehera, I wish you and Hussain a happy married life. May all your wishes come true. May health, wealth and happiness of all kinds be there with you for your entire lifetime and may your children find the cherished childhood filled with fun and laughter which you had wished for as a child. I pray to Sairam for good health and long life for all your family members. May love keep blooming in your life always.

Meena, it was so lovely talking to you and, " Insha Allah", may this book reach cancer affected patients and provide them with the needed strength to fight the disease with a positive mindset.

POETRY ON BREAST CANCER

In the tender dawn of middle-aged grace,
A woman stood with a gentle smile on her face.
Shadowed by life and fleeting, uncertain trance,
Unaware of the danger, the ill-fated dance

Pink ribbons adorned a world unaware,
Of battles fought silently, of the quiet scare
Her body, a canvas where courage unfurls,
A testament to hope amid challenging swirls

Within her being, a secret did repose,
A silent intruder, as dread shadows arose.
Yet destiny whispered with a soft decree,
Embrace awareness, and set your spirit free.

In the mirror, reflection met revelation.
A warrior awakened to a profound sensation.
Breast cancer and hushed whisper, met with a roar,
As she faced the challenge, she opened a new door.

Mammograms told tales of a story untold,
Of resilience and strength, of a bold spirit.
Early detection, a radiant guiding light,
Navigating her through the harrowing night

The surgeon's hands, both skilled and sincere,
Navigated a labyrinth, conquering fear.
The scars on her chest, not marks of defeat,
But symbols of courage, a victory sweet.

Radiation rays, a tender, healing caress,
Banishing shadows, promoting progress
Chemotherapy's dance, a formidable fight,
Yet her spirit danced, bathed in courageous light.

A voice she became, a beacon of hope,
For others like her, learning to cope
In the symphony of survival, she found her tune.
A melody of strength rises like the moon.

Breast cancer awareness, a lifeline cast,
Saving futures and ensuring no moments pass
In the journey of struggle, a metamorphosis rife,
A woman emerged, embracing a new life.

With ribbons of pink, she wove tales untold.
Of resilience, courage, and newfound gold.
Her spirit, unbroken, soared to new heights.
A testament to early detection as a profound lights

Let the world hear; let the banners twirl.
The power of awareness is for every girl.
In the symphony of courage, let their voices sing.
Breast cancer awareness, an anthem echoing

In the tapestry of trials, a resilient thread
Woven by courage, where once fear tread
With ribbons of pink, stories unfold.
Of battles fought bravely, of hearts made bold

Breast cancer awareness, a lifeline cast,
Saving futures and ensuring no moments pass
In the journey of struggle, a metamorphosis rife,
A woman emerged, embracing a new life.

The scars on her chest, not marks of defeat,
But symbols of triumph are sweet.
Her spirit unbroken, soaring to heights,
A beacon for others in their challenging fights.

With voices united, banners unfurled,
The power of awareness is for every girl.
In the symphony of courage, their voices sing.
Breast cancer awareness: a lasting spring

So let the world listen; let the echoes resound.
In the hearts of survivors, hope is found.
For in the face of darkness, a radiant beam,
A testament to strength, an inspiring theme

Dr. Shruti Jha

THE STORY OF SALONI LAKHANI

The most common cause of death all across the globe is breast cancer other than lung, colon, rectum and prostate cancer as per the data provided by The World Health Organization. In India breast cancer is a major public health concern accounting for about twenty eight percent of the total cancer cases which is posing a great public health concern and economic burden on the patients and their families for affording the cost of treatment as per the article written by Pillai, R. N. et al.

The most common risk factors are family history of breast cancer or any case of cancer in the family which requires screening from an early age and even requires genetic testing. Advancing age of conception,untreated infections of breast like breast abscess equally pose a risk of breast cancer in future.

Nulliparity,alcohol,smoking,absence of breastfeeding also increases the risk of cancer. The patients who present with signs and symptoms of breast cancer often present with the following features.

There were many who survived the disease and went back to normal life, however, there are yet others who succumbed to the disease and lost their lives. Like all other cancers the identification of the disease at the right time and the treatment henceforth from competent hands of a doctor are extremely important for the survival of a patient.

It was in the year 2012 I was detected with urinary bladder cancer. I had just shifted to Anand Gujarat and within four days of my arrival one day late at night when I went to the bathroom and I saw I had urinated a huge amount of blood along with the urine. This happened twice and it scared the wits out of me. Within a few visits to the doctor and the screenings which took place I was detected with urinary bladder cancer. I was in a mental and physical state of shock. My treatment and recovery was extremely painful mentally and physically. Slowly with the passage of time I recovered and life limped back to normalcy. In this period I came across many people who were new to me and tried to get me into a normal frame of mind. Socially the ladies who lived nearby tried to cheer me up telling me stories of revival to help me see hope and life post the disease. One among them was Saloni Lakhani who was a neighbour with a heart of gold.

In the year 2014 I had completely come out of the episode of cancer and my life social circle had widened. Saloni, a quiet lady in her forties, a homemaker and a great human being became a good friend of mine. Her husband Vivek worked in the same department and were good colleagues. Vivek and Saloni are blessed with two beautiful and intelligent children. Both children were grown up, daughter a Chartered Accountant was employed with a multinational and son was a student of the National Law School at Gandhinagar. My family's association with the family was heartfelt and small meetings with them gave us a lot of pleasure.

The family was medically aware and went for medical screenings every year. They never missed their dates with their doctor. I had got to know that Saloni was facing a lot of physical pain which she could not recognise any reason for the pain she was going through. She was a member of my reiki group. I remember going to her place to ask regarding her health along with friends when she missed Reiki sessions. She had made frequent visits to the hospital but got no relief from the pain. She wanted to visit an Ayurvedic center to get relief. The ayurvedic treatment actually helped her and she became much better.

All was going well and Saloni was convinced that all physical ailments had been taken care of. She recalled that she needed to get her breast checked by the doctor as two small lumps had appeared on it. This was not the first time the lumps had appeared on her breast. Earlier even a mammogram report had been taken of the lumps and they were found to be water cysts. They used to disappear all by itself in a period of time. They usually appeared around the time her periods were about to break. The first time she had seen the lump she had become extremely upset seeing the lump.

It was the time for the yearly screening and again the lumps were there on her breasts. It was important for her to run the medical tests as usual as it was told by the doctor to her. Saloni was brave and got her breast examined by the doctor. On examination the doctor recommended that she should go through the tests and the mammogram report was necessary. When the results were brought to the doctor the couple was shocked beyond belief that Saloni was suffering from Breast Cancer. She was already on stage 2 and it had affected the lymph nodes.

Catastrophe hit the couple. Both children were in their respective places for work. The couple could not understand the reason for this deadly disease. She had been a strong advocate of home cooked food and led a normal home maker's life. Saloni was a great cook and we all used to love the food she used to make for her family and friends. She kept wondering for days what went wrong as there was no history of cancer in her family. She remained muted for many days and then took charge of the situation. She decided to get rid of the organ so that she could be with her family members. She had seen the doctor's expression. He wanted her to come to a conclusion with her decision at the earliest. So it was decided that mastectomy would necessarily be a part of the procedure and it would be done at the earliest.

Under the supervision of Dr. Srinivasan, her oncologist, a PET scan was conducted to check how far the cancer had spread into the body. The family was relieved to see that the spread was just in the region of the breast. This slightly calmed their nerves. The oncologist saw no reason as to why the process should be delayed. She was immediately sent to an oncologist surgeon at the Sterling hospital by the name of Dr. Somesh Chandra who was working with the Sterling Hospital.

Saloni along with Vivek met Dr. Chandra to discuss the date of the surgery. There were two ways in which the surgery could be approached: one was complete removal of the breast and the second was to remove the affected part of the breast. Given the choices Saloni decided to think it through for a while. The surgeon empathised with her situation and explained to her that one of the major works of this organ is to feed new born babies. It has already done its job. For her safety and to keep the disease at bay it would be best to remove the affected organ. He told her he was completely okay with any decision that she took.

Saloni wanted to inform her family about the new development. She still had not informed her children about the disease as it would bring in a tempest in their life. Post the information both children came down from Mumbai and Ahmedabad respectively. The children were extremely brave and stood by their mother with a great amount of strength. Vivek stood bravely by the side of his wife and children and did not budge from the side of his wife through this entire challenging time that Saloni went through.

As the day of the surgery came in, Saloni was slightly nervous. She was accompanied by all her family members to the surgery room.

As the sun rose on the day of surgery, Saloni, accompanied by her loved ones, arrived at the hospital. The atmosphere was a mix of nervous anticipation and hopeful prayers. The surgical procedure lasted for two hours, during which her family anxiously waited, clinging onto the movement of the clock.

The surgery took nearly two hours and post the surgery it was sometime later that Saloni was shifted to the room. When she regained consciousness it was a great relief to find her family in the room. A mixed emotional moment was flowing in the room. The coming days were not going to be easy. Saloni would have to show a lot of resilience to get back on her feet. There was physical and emotional discomfort initially. After four days in the hospital, she was shifted to her parents' place in Ahmedabad, where their tender care provided solace and reassurance.

After ten days Saloni went back to the hospital. The stitches had to be removed. The doctor was amazed to see her smile and talk to them with full self confidence. The doctor understood that his patient was ready to move ahead with the second level of the treatment. The best part of her treatment was the unwavering support of her family. Saloni had come back to Anand and she was always backed by some family members for support. Her chemo sessions had started and they were painful which goes without a doubt. She suffered from nausea and weakness continuously. However, her family members never let her feel lonely nor did they allow her to feel depressed and miserable with pain.

The family together made the home a place where health was priority and love poured all the time without disruption. There was not just one person who came up to look after Saloni. Members of the family took turns and came in for short and long term periods, not leaving sick Saloni lonely even for a moment. The result was even though her pain was a torture but internally she flourished in the love and attentionshe got. Nothing happened all of a sudden, her process of gaining back strength was a slow and steady process.

Chemotherapy like most patients was tough on Saloni. The pain she encountered was mindless. The burning sensation in the body and the constipation was tough to handle. She was given medicine by her doctor to ease out the situation but chemo sessions are tough on patients. I can speak from my own experience. Here I would like to put into perspective for all my readers that love and affection raises the bar of the emotional quotient which raises resilience in people.

The chemo sessions seem as if they are a never ending toil on the body. With the conclusion of the sessions Saloni took a sigh of relief that this arduous journey was finally coming to an end. Time had tested her resilience towards pain. She was given a brief time to recover from the pain and then her radio therapy sessions started. With renewed strength and zeal Saloni embarked on a new battle to fight the pain and discomfort which would come along with the radio sessions. This took place at Apollo Ahmedabad in which she went through 25 radiation cycles.

The radio therapies were not too long; they were for just four minutes. There was immense emotional turbulence which she faced during her radio sessions. When I spoke to her she told me that she was so scared with the idea of going through the radio sessions that when she actually went through it, the experience was not as painful as her thought. Apollo Ahmedabad treated their patients with great care and ensure their comfort through professional hands. Like always her family was there with her all the time be it her parents, her brother his wife or her children. Everyone took turns and was there by her side.

There is one truth about cancer which is true for all survivors. The disease leaves such a deep mark in your mind and body that one might not forget for their entire life. The entire process of surgery, chemo and radiation left a deep impact on the mind and body of Saloni. The area affected by treatment took on a deep, black hue, a stark reminder of the battle that raged within her body. Yet, as the months unfolded, a gradual transformation occurred. The darkness receded, giving way to renewed vitality and a return to normalcy.

After some time had lapsed a PET scan was conducted to check how effective the treatment had been. There was no trace of Cancer cells in her body. She breathed with ease when the result was told to her. The pain, her resilience and the resolute behaviour had all paid off at the end. Her journey though painful was slowly showing signs of revival and things getting back to normalcy.

Saloni had always been regular with her follow ups. So she was put through X-rays, sonography, blood tests and regular check ups to ensure that her journey against cancer moves without disruption.She was called up to check us after every three months. The people in the medical fraternity were exhilarated to watch her steady progress back to health and reassured her that she was on the right trajectory to recovery.

It is quite understandable that people going through this disease face low immunity for most part of their life or as long as they live. As an immediate effect there is loss of hair which can be witnessed in most patients. The amount of love and compassion which was given to her gave her the strength to fight back against all odyssey stacked up against her.

Saloni was and is a fighter. She is back to Anand in her abode to where she belongs. Vivek had made this house for his beautiful wife with a lot of love and affection. As she entered her home she saw the hopeful eyes of her children and family members who sat back in relief when they knew that no traces of the disease was left inside her. A patient has to undergo a period of darkness during their recovery period. Saloni too had bravely fought this disease with the hope that one day she would be able to appreciate little things around her, live and connect with her loved one and thank god for the little miracles which keep happening around us.

Rendezvous With Saloni Lakhani

Saloni do you think Karma makes people go through such dreadful disease?

I am no authority to talk about Karma. I am a simple housewife. I have led a good life with my husband and children. Everybody has challenges in life and so did I. I think we should treat a disease like a disease. Nothing more than that.

You are an excellent house wife with above average culinary skills. You eat most of the time at home. Then why do you think a person like you suffered with this disease?

The development of society has exposed us to a lot of pollution. One of the major pollutants we are exposed to is the use of disinfectants and insecticides used while growing food. While many think about Karma, I think about the quality of food we get from the market. There is a lot of rise in cancer cases across the country. One of the major reasons for mutation of the cell is the quality of food we eat.

How should the family react when they get to know that a dear person is affected by the disease?

A family is the backbone for any person going through sickness. This was a bitter battle I fought with cancer. The only reason why I was able to do it was because my parents and my elder brother and his wife took turns to take care of me. When neither were there then my children and my husband took leaves to take care of me. Post my chemo period my reiki friends came down to give me reiki so that I could combat the pain. I am lucky I was showered with love and affection. When you are sick people around you should make you feel wanted. Otherwise it is very easy to slip into the gallows of darkness.

Any message you would like to give to my readers?

When you find somebody really sick, help them without thinking about what you would get in return. If it is a loved one who is sick, show them your concern and your love. It is only human. This will give them the strength to fight the pain and get back to health.

Dearest Saloni you are a very dear friend and I have and will always pray for the good health of you and your family. May your abode always shine with the love and affection which your family showers at you. May Lord Sai Nath Maharaj bless you with a long healthy life and may all your dreams come true.

THE STORY OF OVARIAN CANCER

Introduction

A woman is often considered a form of energy, as per Indian mythology termed "Shakti. " She is always regarded as complete in every sense. She has the power to grow life inside her and give birth to a bundle of joy through her womb. The seed of life, a microscopic egg, is released during the ovulation phase of the menstrual cycle. Basically, every month, the body of a female prepares the reproductive system to be conducive for conception. An almond-shaped reproductive organ has a superpower to orchestrate a multitude of phenomena with utmost ease in a coordinated manner. In a way, an average woman balances her personal, professional, and family dynamics with utmost ease. The biology of a woman's genitourinary system creates perfect harmony in her life.

Anatomy of the Seedbank of Joy

It is often said that eating soaked almonds improves memory and strength. Now, what if I present to you the fact that nearly millions of ova are stored in an almond-sized ovary of a woman during fetal development, continuing shortly after birth. The primary oocyte gets arrested in the diplotene phase of Meiosis I. One can clearly imagine that nearly 1 million ova are in store until the girl reaches puberty. By that time, many ova have transformed from the primary oocyte to the secondary oocyte phase, where they undergo maturation and are released into the uterus. Every month, from the time a girl reaches puberty, there is development of primary and secondary sexual characteristics. Namely, this includes the maturation of the mammary glands, axillary and pubic hair growth, voice changes, growth spurts, and female patterns of weight gain. The hormones stimulating the release of oocytes create such a significant change in the human body.

The ovary weighs 4-8 grams and measures about 35mm x 25mm x 18mm in dimension at the time of puberty, which regresses at menopause with a volume of 8ml. This organ is attached to the fallopian tube and uterus by the paraoophoron, epoophoron, hydatid of Morgagni, and the ovarian ligament.

Ovarian Tumour

Introduction

It is the malignant transformation of normal ovarian tissue into cancerous tissue under the influence of the suppression of tumor suppressor markers and increased levels of certain tumor activators after one achieves puberty.

Incidence

Ovarian tumor is the seventh most common type of tumor and the second most common type of cancer globally and in India, respectively. India has nearly 47,000 cases and 39,000 deaths, mainly due to the detection of cases at advanced stages.

Aetiology

It is the most common cause of mortality among women, diagnosed at a late presentation between the ages of 45 and 60 years. Women who have not conceived, consume a high- calorie and high-fat diet, have a previous history of polycystic ovarian syndrome, experience late menopause, have a family history of breast and gastrointestinal cancer, possess a genetic predisposition due to BRCA-1 and BRCA-2 gene mutations, and undergo multiple cycles of ovulation induction are factors that increase the risk of ovarian cancer.

Pathogenesis

Long- standing untreated pre-malignant conditions, stressors, and a sedentary lifestyle lead to the expression of tumor factors and the suppression of tumor-suppressing genes, resulting in a multitude of ovarian cancers which is presented at later stages.

Clinical feature

The symptoms are nonspecific in the early stages, leading to late diagnosis. The tumor presents bilaterally. In the early stages, the patient would be asymptomatic. Initially, the patient would present with abdominal fullness after meals, changes in bowel habits, or generalized pain in the abdomen mimicking gastrointestinal symptoms, which causes patients to visit surgeons and medical practitioners instead of the gynecologist. There have been cases where right iliac fossa pain could be a ruptured ectopic in the ovary or ovarian torsion, which are gynecological emergencies. These should always be kept in mind apart from the gastrointestinal symptoms. Regular visits to the gynecologist can reduce this confusion. In malignant ovarian tumors, the patient can also present with fluid accumulation in the abdomen, unilateral fluid accumulation that is non-pitting edema, and an enlarged liver. If there are palpable lymph nodes and palpable nodules on pelvic examination, along with fluid accumulation in the lung cavity leading to difficulty in breathing, these are suggestive of advanced malignancy. At every stage, there are multiple differential diagnoses considered while diagnosing a case of ovarian tumor. It is exceptionally tricky, as it mimics multiple gastrointestinal diseases, causing diagnosis in later stages when there is metastasis. At the stage of metastasis, fatigability, weakness, cachexia, and bone pain are also symptoms seen in such patients.

Investigation

Ultrasound shows a solid tumor with echogenic or cystic areas, a thick capsule with papillary projections, and a thick septum measuring more than 5 mm in a malignant tumor. The tumor where the ovary has malignancy is enlarged, or a bilateral tumor can be found. On endometrial biopsy, if the endometrial thickness is more than 4 mm with papillary projections in a perimenopausal woman. In case of a tumor, CA-125 has a differential diagnosis of both ovarian tumor and peritoneal tuberculosis, so clinical correlation is extremely essential with the case history of the patients. CT and MRI indicate the extent of the tumor's spread. A barium meal, barium enema, and breast examination are required when metastatic tumors are suspected ; X-ray of the chest and liver scan are necessary to detect metastatic growth. Doppler ultrasound showing a low pulsatile index of less than 0.4 suggests malignancy. In malignant tumors, new blood vessel formation is often noticed. Patients who are postmenopausal and perimenopausal women with postmenopausal bleeding should undergo dilatation and curettage. CEA greater than 5 micrograms /mL is reported to have an increased risk of ovarian tumors. CT and MRI are useful in determining lymph nodal enlargement and metastatic lesions.

Treatment

If the tumor is restricted to only one ovary, then conservative surgery can be performed, which involves the removal of one or both ovaries and the Fallopian tube, with the conservation of the uterus in case the patient was detected at an early stage with no metastasis and the woman is nulliparous. In such cases, if women remain disease-free for a span of 2 years with one ovary preserved, then she can try spontaneously or by IVF. In case of advanced ovarian cancer, one should always keep in mind that in the presence of metastasis and advanced metastatic lesions, debulking surgery should be performed along with chemotherapy, which consists of the removal of the ovary, Fallopian tubes, uterus, and lymph nodes, along with chemotherapy post-surgery.

Prevention

One should always keep in mind that ovarian malignancy has a high risk of recurrence. Maintaining a healthy lifestyle with a low-calorie, high -fiber, high-protein diet can help achieve a good weight. A patient with a palpable ovary, a history of PCOS, OCP, and the presence of a palpable ovary should be considered for regular follow-up and have regular surveillance every six months. The patient with postmenopausal bleeding should also be under regular surveillance. Women should lead an active lifestyle and, most importantly, stay in regular contact with their gynecologist. Nowadays, the easy accessibility of specialists in tier 1 and tier 2 cities makes it extremely convenient for women to undergo full-body checkups in government and private setups because these cancers are often diagnosed accidentally in scenarios where the patient presents with one complaint but ends up having this disease.

Winning over disease is like winning a battle in life. In our lives, we encounter multiple challenges, some financial, spiritual, physical, mental, and even health -related. The fighting spirit and resilience are qualities that should not be lost. Never be vulnerable to any situation under any circumstances. The same principle can be applied to this notorious disease, which is difficult to diagnose and has a high rate of recurrence ; a doctor can help alleviate the symptoms and troubles. Keeping hope during such trying times, with timely diagnosis and intervention, can prevent the risk of morbidity and mortality. Attenders and family members are encouraged, to spend time with them, help them, and support them. Undergoing the treatment of cancer is more like an ordeal or a transformative journey. They are asked to maintain a stress-free environment for them and be a source of hope, which helps patients fight the disease.

During a war, when one looks at both warring parties or even in a court case, sometimes, more than accuracy, it is the confidence that the client has in the lawyer that encourages them to go the extra mile to win the case. Similarly, if the patient remains faithful to their clinician and vice versa, along with resilience and a fighting spirit from the family, it motivates the doctor to also go the extra mile for them. During the cancer journey, the best teacher for a doctor is their patient, as each case is akin to an encyclopedia of information which is put to test. The patient should always keep their doctor informed for follow-up checkups post-treatment. Their family members should also be informed, and if possible, they should visit the gynecologist if similar symptoms develop. At the end of the day, a single case of cancer not only affects the individual but also impacts the family of the patient and the people around them, as they are also part of the journey. They are passively part of your struggle, so never feel all alone. Your hope and resilience will not only make an impact on you but also on others around you. If you maintain this fighting spirit, even a battle with a notorious tumor like this is achievable.

THE STORY OF MONALBEN AND VISHAD SHAH

Hold on to your heart. When you read this story, you will start believing that God, who is a formless bundle of energy, comes to your rescue in various forms. Especially when children suffer, God sends white-winged angels wearing white coats to save you.

Om Sai Ram, Sai Baba, please hold my pen and strengthen my fingers, and let the pain I hear not weaken me and my senses. After listening to this story, my belief in your grace has increased tenfold. After remembering your kind and graceful feet, I am beginning this story.

Chintanbhai, Monalben, and their son Vishad held on to their belief in wellness and life by doing their seva to Lord Mahavir and believing in his teachings. They recall the entire story, which they went through bravely with smiles on their faces. Chintan Bhai says it was Lord Mahavir and the prayers of his family that helped them endure so much pain, and even today, he can share a smile with his wife and son, whom he loves and cherishes.

In December 2003, the little boy Vishad found himself facing a battle he never expected. The story of Vishad started when his parents noticed red- colored urine in the pot. It was a strange experience for the family, peculiar but insignificant in detail, so they decided to bring it to the attention of a medical practitioner. They had no idea that it would be the beginning of a life-altering journey.

Like all parents, Vishad's parents worried about the little boy's food intake. Of late, the intake had drastically reduced. Somehow, it came to their minds to get a sonography done for the child. There were some puzzles around the little child's health that needed decoding. The doctor didn't say much but recommended a CT scan for the child.

Chintan Shah, Vishad's father, was being guided by his first cousin, Dr. Meeta Shah, in the process. Dr. Shah wanted the family to consult a specialist and referred them to Dr. Desai, who is a famous urologist at Muljibhai Hospital. Dr. Desai went through all the reports, conducted a few tests himself, and informed the family that there was a small tumor in the kidney, which was the cause of the malfunction of the organ. The family was shocked beyond imagination. Dr. Desai expressed confidence in his treatment of Vishad, believing that the disease could be managed effectively.

To understand the process of treatment, a renal scan was done for Vishad. This provided them with the output for each kidney. Since the child was under seven years old, the best surgeons at Muljibhai were involved in his treatment. The doctors took care to ensure that the little boy received the utmost attention, considering his tender age throughout the treatment period.

To decide how to best treat the kidney, a nephrologist from the hospital also joined the team. It was the teamwork of the doctors that seemed to provide hope to the ailing child and his family.

The doctors decided that little Vishad would undergo chemotherapy sessions. The sessions were designed to suit the age of the little boy. On the 1st of January, Vishad was admitted to the hospital for the sessions. To counter the pain, breaks were given to the child from the chemotherapy during the time frame when he was allowed to go back to his own home to recuperate from the pain. This went on for two months, with CT scans being done on the child to check the size of the tumor and see if there was any change in its size.

There were two things that worried Vishad's family. One was the financial implications of fighting the disease, and the other was the risk of infections during the hospitalization process. Dr. Mahesh Desai was extremely sensitive regarding Vishad's age. A different bed was made for Vishad to suit his age in the post-operative ward. The compassion shown by the doctors was beyond comprehension.

The little boy was going through a grueling time in his life. It was not easy for him. The chemotherapy sessions were making a heavy impact on his body. Twice during that period, the little child was admitted to the hospital for high fever. Throughout this entire process, while the parents were battling for Vishad's life, all relatives and friends rallied to the hospital to visit the little boy to meet and entertain him. There was a tremendous emotional and physical strain the couple was experiencing for their child.

Following the chemotherapy, the child was given a two -month break during which they went home. After the break, Dr. Desai recommended surgery to remove the tumor. Initially, the left kidney was treated, and after a period of 20 days, the second kidney was operated on. For 35 days, the little boy battled post-operative discomfort and expressed his frustrations through tantrums and outbursts due to pain, longing to leave the hospital and play like other children. This treatment of Vishad Shah continued until April 2005, at which point he was called for routine check-ups. The empathy and compassion they received at the hospital or from their relatives cannot be described in words.

With the passage of time, people learned about the resilience and brave battle fought by Vishad and his family. This gave strength to them and to others who came in contact with them, showing that any challenge can be defeated if one has the right mindset.

The Story of Monal Shah

Monal, who was Vishad's mother, had been through many anxious times in her life during Vishad's recovery. She was in physical pain and consistently experienced discomfort in the lower part of her stomach.

Monal, who always showered Vishad with love and care, was enduring persistent pain and physical anxiety to which she could not assign a reason. Their lives took an unexpected turn when Monal began experiencing constant pain in the lower part of her abdomen.

One of the major thoughts that crossed her mind was that perhaps she had a gynaecological issue. When the tests and screenings were conducted, a large cyst was found on her right ovary. The doctors wasted no time and immediately scheduled her for surgery. The cyst and the affected ovary were removed. The cyst was sent for biopsy, and the results were awaited. Within a few days, the results were discussed with the Shah family. To their utter dismay and surprise, they discovered that the cyst that had been removed was a malignant growth. Monal had still not recovered from Vishad's ill health and cancer episode; this was a shock for her and her family. It was stage 1 ovarian cancer.

This life-altering diagnosis needed to be addressed with a senior doctor. Monal's husband, Chintanbhai, sought the expertise of Dr. Ketan Shah, a general oncological surgeon, and Dr. Anila Kapadia, an oncological gynaecologist in Ahmedabad. Further investigations were conducted to understand the spread of the disease.

In the subsequent surgery, Monal had her second ovary removed, followed by her uterus, fallopian tubes, omentum, and appendix. Monal was going through a difficult time, but she maintained a brave face for her child and her loving husband. It was a five-day stay at the hospital before she was sent home to recover.

Post- surgery, the chemotherapy cycles began, administered every 21 days. The suffering that follows chemotherapy is common knowledge these days. In the last cycle of chemotherapy, Monal's blood count dropped, so medical intervention was necessary to stabilize her condition. This led to months of physical and emotional pain; however, her treatment eventually came to an end.

Monal was a mindful person. To recover from the effects of chemotherapy, she adopted many healthy practices, such as drinking fresh juices, soups, and regularly consuming jowar water to boost her blood count. She also sought relief from pain through Reiki.

I even remember taking Reiki sessions during my recovery process after chemotherapy. Monal's determination and the support of her family and relatives played a crucial role in her healing. For the next ten years, Monal and Vishad attended regular check-ups, feeling a sense of normalcy in their lives. However, fate had more challenges in store for them, and their strength was again put to test.

Vishads Kidney Transplant

Chintanbhai stood like a tower of strength for his wife and his son. His challenges were not about to get over. For years they went for regular check ups and avoided many medical troubles for the future. There was another war which needed to be fought which would test their resilience.

It was around the year 2017 when Vishad was at the Muljibhai hospital for his checkups. A very high blood pressure was reported which was a point of worry for the doctors. He was referred to the nephrology department for diagnosis. A regular medication was given to Vishad to control his blood pressure.

Another routine checkup for Vishad found a problem with his ureter. This again led the mother and son duo to see Dr. Mahesh Desai. The next day a CT scan was conducted and in the result a growth in the ureter was found. Dr. Desai recommended surgery to investigate the issue further and sent the sample for biopsy. Additionally, a stent was placed in Vishad's kidney to alleviate the situation temporarily.

This surgery was small and it provided the information to the medical fraternity as to how the case should be handled. The biopsy result showed no malignancy which was a relief for the family.Suddenly within days Vishad developed a high fever which just would not abate. The removal of the growth in the ureter and the reinsertion of the stent brought a sudden rise in the creatinine level which was 2.1 which worried the doctors.

The health crisis was unsettling and was a crucial time of his school life who was studying in class 12. Despite the medical challenges, he managed to sit for the class 12 exam. He managed to pass his class 12 exam with 86% marks showing his resilience and absolute belief in himself irrespective of the stumbling block on his way.

Another dramatic event took place and it was found that his creatinine level was at 5 post his exam of class 12th. Dr.

Umapati Hegde, his nephrologist, gave the news to his parents. According to his prediction he told his parents that the creatinine level might rise further. Therefore there was a need for dialysis for Vishad. In November or December, the family fails to recall the exact month; a test revealed that Vishad's creatinine level had reached a distressing 8.

A critical turn came in the life of Vishad and his family as Vishad's creatinine level shot up to an unbelievable number of 13. This was an alarming situation, and the family rushed to Muljibhai to consult Dr. Desai. On January 19, the boy went through his first dialysis session. The treatment did not deter him from attending his college and continuing with his education. The schedule of dialysis was maintained.

The young man went through 54 sessions of dialysis. The resilience of the boy is beyond imagination. Never once has he mentioned his emotional upheaval while relating the story. Another huge factor is the unconditional support of the family during these trying times.

While this challenge was being addressed, two nodules were discovered behind Vishad's left ear in March. Dr. Desai advised the removal of the nodules, as Vishad would soon require a kidney transplant. Monal's mother, Surekha Ben, selflessly agreed to be the kidney donor, offering a glimmer of hope amid the darkness.

Before the transplant could take place, the procedure for removing the nodule was done. The histopathological examination showed early malignancy symptoms. This caused further distress to the couple. Dr. Kaustubh bhai Patel recommended surgery to excise the affected region of the parotid gland. In June 2019, Vishad underwent the surgical procedure in the presence of Dr. Desai, who provided his support and expertise to the doctors throughout the process.

Again, the same old regimen of dialysis continued for a period of two months. Following the surgical procedure, Vishad resumed the demanding regimen of dialysis for a period of two months. The grueling process tested his endurance. In August 2019, Vishad underwent the life-changing kidney transplant procedure, and he became completely healthy, starting to lead a normal life like all other adults of his age.

Post - transplant, Vishad regularly underwent check-ups and adhered to the prescribed medications given by the doctors. This constant watch and intervention by the senior doctors helped his body to heal. After so many health setbacks, he remains focused on his goal to achieve something tangible in his life.

At the age of 23, Vishad looks towards a bright future. He pursues an integrated MBA course at Ahmedabad University. All his friends, colleagues, and professors know him for his tough resilience and resolute behavior. This story was told to me by Dr. Desai during one of the meetings.

As Dr. Desai related the story to me, I was spellbound. It took me back to those days when I was being operated on, and the bed next to me was occupied by a five-year-old girl who had some kidney issue. I was so caught up in my own emotional trauma that I did not understand what was happening around me. My heart went out to Monalben, who must have suffered and died a million deaths during the process of treatment. Seeing a small child go through this kind of trauma is not easy. Tears spilled from my eyes after listening to her story and emotional distress.

Rendezvous with Vishad and Monal Shah

Vishad and Monalben, what have you learned from this long medical journey?

Vishad shared how his medical challenges had shaped him into a compassionate and target-driven individual. His journey had taught him the value of empathy, the strength of human connection, and the importance of never giving up.

He wanted to live and achieve for his family. The strength in his voice was due to the raw pain which he had gone through from his childhood. I saw the strength of character, and the determination to achieve from his resolute behaviour and aura. I made up my mind to write about him and his family. There are people who are ill with terminal illness and this story would add to their willingness to fight back.

Vishad, what would you like to achieve in the future?

The state of Gujarat is filled with aspiring entrepreneurs. One day he would like to embark on this journey and set up his own venture.

I wish Monalben and Vishad all the very best in life. May they have great health and a long life. May all their dreams be fulfilled. One thing I am very sure of is that Vishad will grow up to be an empathetic human being. People like him are truly needed in society.

One day, I would want to see him on a chat show on television or read his success story in a glossy magazine as one of the bright young entrepreneurs of Gujarat -a warrior with a heart of gold. I pray to Sairam for the good health of Chintanbhai's family and the professional success of Vishad in achieving his dream.

Now let me tell you another story of a scholarly young man who shared his story and war against the deadly disease of Cancer.

STORY OF PROFESSOR DR. GOKUL

The story, which I am about to relate, has its roots in the vibrant city of Hyderabad. Today, the city is well known for its cosmopolitan culture; however, it also has a rich cultural heritage, which gives it a perfect blend of old traditions and the modern values of the current generation. Dr. Gokul, who is currently working as a professor with IIT Kanpur, a very learned man, I was lucky to interact with, while searching for the next story for my book. He happened to be a colleague of my husband's friend, and he agreed to share his story for my readers.

Dr. Gokul belongs to the Lambadi tribal community of Rajasthan. It is a migrating tribe, and their forefathers migrated from Rajasthan and settled in a village that is 60 km away from Hyderabad around 200 years ago. The name of the village is Jajiguda Tanda, near Kodicherla village, Kothur, Ranga Reddy District, in the state of Telangana. He was born in Bapu Nagar, Hyderabad. He talks very fondly about his childhood, which he shared with his two brothers. An energetic boy right from the start, he excelled in both academics and physical strength. He completed his karate brown belt during his school days. His father and mother were both working individuals, and the home was a strong abode of love and affection. He says he grew up eating the traditional food of his tribe as well as enjoying Hyderabadi cuisine. He can speak his mother tongue and uses a typical Marwari dialect when he speaks.

His father, Mr. Shridhar, retired as a master craftsman from Hindustan Machines and Tools, Chintal, Balanagar, Telangana. His mother, Ms. Radha, retired as District Panchayat Officer, Mahbubabad District, Telangana. He enjoyed his childhood with his two siblings, Madhava and Keshava. Their childhood was healthy and lively. He says all members of his family are well-educated and employed in government jobs. When I asked him to define himself as an individual, he said he is a global citizen even though he had never traveled abroad. He chuckles and laughs while talking. He said he needed to correct that in the near future after making this statement.

His earliest memories of childhood involve traveling to his native village where the family would gather to celebrate Dussehra. The family would be busy with festivity and feasting all the while ; however, what he enjoyed the most was the dance performed by the ladies at night in traditional folklore. I asked him if it was something like Garba ; he denied and said it was a slow dance unique to their community. Dr. Gokul speaks proudly about his community. Since it was a nomadic community, the food they ate was very traditional, and because they were always on the move, most people were fit as a fiddle, with a normal life expectancy of around 80 to 100 years. The food consisted mainly of roti made from jowar flour and fresh vegetables, along with lentils, which were incredibly healthy.

After his schooling, he pursued a degree in Biomedical Engineering from Osmania College, after which he joined IIT Kanpur for his MBA. As he recalls his college days, he has a clear remembrance of all 23 friends who graduated with him. All of them had taken the GRE exam, qualified, and went abroad for further education. Even though he had taken the exam and qualified, he could not avail himself of the opportunity due to a financial crunch at home, so he decided to take up a job for himself.

Therefore, he joined a company named Rashtriya Ispat Nigam Limited in Vizag. He joined as a Technical Assistant to the Director of Finance. This role gave him a lot of power, and he enjoyed it for a period of one year. However, after that year, he decided to request a transfer from Vizag to Delhi. After a period of six months, he chose to completely quit his job as he did not enjoy what he was doing. He went back home and started preparing for the UPSC exam. He cleared the Mains exam, but could not clear the interview. It was around this time that his marriage was fixed, and he got settled in life.

The Bank Recruitment test went well, and he was selected as a Management Executive, working with them for a period of one and a half years. Banking jobs are very hectic ; he says especially his experience in the Rural Credit Processing Cell with SBI was extremely exhaustive. He was appreciated for his commendable work, but internally he missed seeing the sunset in the evening, as he was always overworked until late evening and too tired all the time. It was in the midst of this period that his eldest son, Venu, was born. Torn between the need to spend some quality time with his family, he decided to quit his job when he moved to Suryapet. His stint with SBI lasted for a period of 2.5 years. All well-wishers asked him not to leave, but he had made up his mind to move on for good.

He finally decided to get back to college and complete his Doctoral program. He needed to qualify the CAT or NET exam before choosing any university. He qualified both the exams and he got a call from many prestigious universities like IITs and IIM's. Finally he chose IIM Shillong for his Doctoral program in the year 2013. It was around this time his second son Vedant was born. He remembers Shillong with a sense of awe, as one of the most beautiful places in India. Up in the hills it seems as if one is living with the clouds he says. Northeast has been highly underrated by our people. That is the place to holiday as it is one of the most beautiful places in the world. The cleanliness, the civic sense of the locals and the pristine beauty makes it like a heaven on earth.

The doctoral program was for around five years and Dr. Gokul was too immersed and busy sheafing through the pages of the book. He was not worried about his family, as back in Hyderabad his parents and his brother's family all stayed in the same building along with his family. However, what he did not know was the fact that there was a storm brewing back home. The pressure of submitting his thesis was on the rise and there was pressure building up from his wife to leave his thesis and come back home. Initially he tried to calm it down however one day he got to know that his wife had taken both his children and left for her mothers place. A sad unpleasantness started to grow inside him and to keep his concentration at his work he got back to smoking cigarettes which he had left before his marriage. In the times which lay ahead Dr. Gokul started getting bouts of dry cough after every six to seven months. Many tests were performed and ultrasound was done however nothing was found. In the year 2018 he submitted his thesis and his doctoral program came to an end.

In the year 2019 he was called by a private university to join as an Assistant. Professor which was located in Kamalghat near Agartala, Tripura. Like all private jobs this was again a heavy toll job loaded with responsibilities. There was the work of teaching several batches plus other administrative work which needed to be completed through the day. He stayed there for a period of six to seven months and then quit his job and started to apply for other new upcoming IIMs. His marriage was getting worse by the day. One day his wife's parents created a huge commotion at his house in Hyderabad due to which they finally decided to go ahead with the process of divorce. Meanwhile Dr. Gokul was intermittently meeting the doctors for the dry cough which was a consistent worry for him.

In the year 2019, one day he received a call from Ravindra Global University to join as a Professor for Marketing Research. He immediately moved to Gaya, and recalls that he joined the university in the morning and in the evening on the same day he had taken a class. He smiles at his recollection. An immediate feedback was taken post the class and he got excellent scores. He joined the university as an Asst. Professor and Chairperson MDP and Consultancy. In December 2020 he decided to move closer to his home and applied for Vedanta National University. This was not taken in good taste by the management and his candidature was rejected due to a negative feedback from the college.

Dr. Gokul immediately resigned and left for home. Covid was already in and raging by that time. Just around the same time both children of Dr. Gokul were sent back by his wife to Hyderabad. This was done to discomfort the family however it gave immense pleasure to him to welcome the kids back in his abode. It was Dr. Gokul's habit, to burn camphor in the morning and evening during the puja. Suddenly one day he felt that he had no sense of smell and taste. He and his younger son were already running a temperature so he decided to get himself tested. Both tested positive for Covid. Both were put in isolation and they recovered after a few days. He took along with him the medicine prescribed by doctors, a Unani medicine called Zinda Tilismath for recovery.

In the year 2023 Dr. Gokul joined IIT Kanpur as a Professor for Marketing Research. After a period of one month he suffered from a high grade fever of 103 - 105 degree which refused to abate. He was admitted to the Regency hospital. His blood parameters were abnormal and he felt extremely unwell. He informed his college regarding his health condition and left for Hyderabad. A bone marrow test was performed on him and he was detected with Acute Myeloid Leukemia. Immediately his Head of the Department was informed. He was admitted at AIG Hospital for chemotherapy. Over a period of time the effect of the chemo was such that the upper layer of his skin from head to toe peeled off. During the second round of chemo while coming out of the bathroom he slipped and his head hit the floor. He was rushed to the hospital with a Hemorrhage. This happened just the next day after he got discharged from the hospital, after the second round of chemo (On Daunorubicin + Cytarabine). Craniotomy was performed the very same day, He was comatose for 2 days, and on the third day he came out of coma. He got discharged after a week, and after 6 weeks he again got admitted to the hospital for Cranioplasty, he was again hospitalised for one week. Each round of chemo was costing him Rs. 12 lakh. This not only blew up his own savings but also the savings of his loved ones. He immediately realised that he would need to stop the chemo sessions and move to oral medication. He had now been away from college for a period of ten months now and he decided to join back work and get back to normal life.

Along with the college he continued with his oral medication which was tough to handle. The effect of the medication was such that his mouth was devoid of the saliva and there was a constant puking sensation and he puked 7-8 times a day. It was in April 2024 that the court agreed to grant Dr. Gokul and his wife a divorce and in July their marriage was annulled. Now he works for IIT Kanpur, and leads a normal life. The golden lining in his life are his parents and his two children who have grown up much before their age and understand the condition of their father. He remembers his second chemo session in which his eldest son volunteered to be by his side in the hospital to take care of him. He tells me, "My eldest son is not a child anymore, he is already a man who is taking up responsibilities. He stayed in the hospital for a period of one month with me during my second chemo session. I am looking forward to spending time with my sons and we are going to take care of each other. My eldest son has even learnt how to cook so he is more than capable when compared to children of his own age." My eyes misted as I was reminded of my eldest daughter who had to try her hands on cooking when I was getting treated at the hospital for Bladder Cancer. Life is unpredictable and how it would turn out the next second is hard to predict. It is only with the help of God's blessings and the blessings of the people we love we can hope to have a better tomorrow. I really hope deep in my heart that God weeds out all difficulties from his life and gives a fulfilled tomorrow. Days filled with the smiles of his children and full of energy and health. I wish him all the best and hope all his aspirations are achieved and he gets the peace and accomplishment he has been looking for.

Rendezvous With Dr. Gokul

The entire story of Dr. Gokul came to an end. The only thing I felt was that he was incredibly brave to have battled one situation after another, all coming sequentially into his life. There was an unsettled silence at both ends. Then I decided to push in my next set of questions to him.

How do you perceive the disease Cancer?

He thought for a while and then came up with an answer. He said, "It is a disease of consciousness. This disease builds when one puts their body in an uncomfortable state for a prolonged period of time. Usually, people equate cancer with food, which is not right. However, when I look at my life, I feel dejected about many things. Among other things, I feel that due to the community I come from, I had to work twice as much as other people to get where I am. There have been many stressful moments in my life." Coming from an academician, I would not even doubt the authenticity of his statement. However, thoughts started to swirl in my mind. Life usually does not give us the luxury of opting out of a situation all the time. The stress in personal and professional lives is so high that cancer has become a common disease.

Now that you are leading a normal life, how has your health been on an everyday basis?

Dr. Gokul answered meticulously. "I am always low on energy. I always save up my energy so that I can take my classes."

What would you like to tell other people who are confronting this disease?

His voice was full of pain, and he hurried with his answer. "I do not want to confront such people ever in my life. One of my guides at my PhD college was diagnosed with Stomach Cancer. He passed away within a period of four months. People feel that nothing can happen to them; however, this is a myth. Anyone can go through this disease, and there is no set lifestyle to stop this disease."

What are the most blissful moments of your life?

"My father is my hero," he says with a smile. "He stood like an unwavering pillar of strength in all the ordeals that I went through." He laughs and says that he resembled a Telugu actor and that he was the most handsome man of his life. Helping my sons with their studies and spending time with them is when I am the most elated.

I could not help smiling at Dr. Gokul's honest confession. Finally, I needed to close the conversation, and I said, "Sir, I wish you and your family bliss from the depths of my heart. You have been through extremely trying times; however, time and love have their healing effects, which we cannot ignore. In the company of your children, you will find delight and pleasure in your abode. I will pray to Sai Maharaj for you and your family's good health and happiness."

AN ODE TO ORAL CANCER

Oral Cavity

In the journey of human evolution, the key differentiating feature between a man and an animal is the fact that there is an increase in the size of the brain and cranium cavity. The gastrointestinal system developed as the human discovered fire and started eating meat cooked from fire as a source and not being solely dependent on raw food which is difficult to eat and digest. This mere change created a landslide change in the evolution of human beings.

Introduction

Oral cavity mainly consist of cheek, hard palate, soft palate, tongue, tonsil, teeth along with the muscle of chewing and mastication, lips along with mandible and maxilla. In India oral cancer is one of the most common types of cancer which is widely affecting both male and females. The most leading cause of morbidity, mortality and causing debilitating effects on patients.

Aetiology

The main cause of oral cancer is oral tobacco chewing, working on tobacco field, lack of hygiene, absence of washing of hands after working in the tobacco field and eating food as the particles gets accumulated in the oral cavity in the respiratory tract and oral cavity. These are the leading causes of oral cancer of women and children. Among men it is due to active smoking and eating betel leaves and chewing along with dry tobacco leaves. The consumption causes recurrent trauma. Apart from this, continuous alcohol consumption is one of the risk factors for this disease. Chronic fungal infections which are long standing in nature in association with sexually transmitted infection due to oral sexual intercourse could also be one of the risk factors for oral carcinoma. Continuous chronic consumption of alcohol is also one of the risk factors as these substances have high alcohol content causing serious damage to the oral cavity.

Chronic vitamin deficiencies like iron and folic acid could also be the risk factor for oral cancer apart from this human papilloma virus could also be a possible cause. Pre-existing premalignant conditions like white deposition of a plaque-like substance over the oral cavity or red plaque-like deposition over the oral cavity are also potential risk factors of oral cancer among non-smokers. Eating hot spicy food and presence of sharp teeth which leads to continuous trauma due to the formation of ulcers in the oral cavity is also one of the risk factors for oral cancer. Low immunity, poor oral and dental hygiene, poor fitting dentures, history of squamous cell carcinoma, diet low in fruits and vegetables, weakened immunity are also considered the risk factors for oral cancer.Often in rural areas it is noticed that women and children are involved in the agricultural sector apart from men. They are mostly involved in the tobacco harvesting sector where the waste of the harvested products are burnt. When the harvested byproducts are burnt, they are passively inhaled in the process of working in the agricultural field which affects their respiratory system and subsequently affecting their digestive system as they consume the food without washing their hands for a long period of time which affects their oral cavity as well.

Pathogenesis

Due to the activation of tumour markers and the suppression of the tumour suppressor genes with recurrent trauma due to the pre existing risk factors causes the risk of developing oral cancer subsequently.

Clinical features

Due to repetitive history of chronic smoking, chewing pan along with slaked lime causes the development of painless ulcers which subsequently becomes painful which causes pain in the oral cavity. The patient also presents with a history of difficulty in chewing difficulty in speech are also important clinical features. The patient will also present with bad odour breath due to the necrosis of the tumour as the common feature in oral cancer. The patient will also present with a locked jaw as the patient is unable unable to eat adequately eventually leads to weight loss. There is a risk of metastasis and secondary lesions beyond the region where the tumour is fixed. It involves lymph nodal enlargement in the oral cavity specifically in the retromolar trigone in the corner of the mouth where the lymph nodes are present causing severe pain to the patient. The symptoms cause psychological trauma to the patient. There are episodes of secondary sepsis and uncontrollable bleeding. The patient presents with upper airway obstruction and broncho pneumonia. The patient also presents with decreased immunity causing the manifestation of these symptoms. There are also features of breathing difficulties. Fatigue and tiredness are also the key features due to difficulty in eating solid food leading to considerable loss of weight. There can be a history of lymph nodal enlargement in the sternocleidomastoid and in the neck region. There can be passage formation via skin and lymph nodes causing the dribbling of saliva. The patient can present these features bilaterally.

Investigation

A detailed history should be taken and considered for all the risk factors for the oral carcinoma. Wedge biopsy of the tissue should be taken from the edge from two sites for histopathological examination to differentiate into well differentiated, moderately, poorly and very poorly differentiated tumours. FNAC should be taken from lymph nodes. CT scan is used to assess the extent of tumour into the mandible, pterygoid region. In patients with lymph nodal involvement CT scan should be done. MRI is very useful in assessing the soft tissue and perineural involvement. Orthopantogram should be done to look for involvement of mandible destruction and fracture sites. The opinion and help of the dentist should also be considered in view of teeth extraction, prosthesis preparation and dentures. PET CT should be done in cases of advanced metastasis. Sentinel lymph node biopsy can be done in case of metastasis.

Treatment

Surgery is often the mainstay of treatment where there is removal of the area where the lesions by wide local excision along with mandible removal along with lymph nodes removal. Radiotherapy can be given palliative or curative or intensity modulated. Chemotherapy which may be IV, oral or intra arterial. Facial reconstruction can be considered. Palliative therapy should also be given to the patient. A multidisciplinary approach is taken between the dentist, surgeon and plastic surgeon. Surgery is indicated in early tumour spreading to the mandible, presence of haemorrhage, recurrence, multiple sites, soft tissue spread and locally advanced but can be removed by surgical method. Pain control, curative and arrest of ulcer and bleeding are the advantages of surgery.

Prevention

Especially in rural areas where there is high cultivation of tobacco. The innocent women and children are often involved in the growth of these crops. While handling these substances at the time of harvesting or while burning the waste or while making the beedi, the use of personal protective equipment should be used namely mask and glove during the working hours in order to reduce the exposure via the aero digestive systems and to reduce the risk of oral, lung cancer. Apart from proper hand hygiene and bathing practice it should be done before and after the exposure of the parts exposed to avoid the tobacco to remain for longer duration. The men should avoid smoking and tobacco chewing in the presence of family members in a public place where there are women and children increasing the risk of carcinoma as they are passively inhaling the same particles as the smoke is experienced in the presence of a person who is actively smoking. The government should take keen interest in banning smoking in public places. The government and health institutions like medical colleges and hospitals should create awareness about the fact to stop smoking in general among the citizens to stop the malpractice in general. If anyone wants to stop smoking or tobacco chewing then the deaddiction centres should support such people in order to prevent oral cancer in the society.

This is far worse than someone who is actively smoking as the person does not have any of effluent filtered when respired passively in comparison to an active smoker who is even though smoking but while puffing out the smoke majority of the smoke particles are removed. The patient should maintain regular dental hygiene. In case of a sharp tooth or an ill fitted dentures should be immediately informed if it causes multiple episodes of trauma. The patient should have adequate hydration.

One should avoid spicy food rather consume food items which have more of a soothing effect on the oral cavity. It is kindly requested to avoid smoking in residential and public premises as the innocent non-smokers should not pay the cost of your addiction by becoming passively smoking plus the law also prohibits smoking in public places. Avoid consuming tobacco and slaked lime rather the measures should be taken to come out of the addiction. One should contact the doctor in the rehabilitation centres to undergo rehabilitation exercise. This small initiative will not only change your life but also the life of your family members. Use of protective equipment like condoms in sexual intercourse and abnormal sexual practices should be avoided to avoid the risk of predisposition of sexually transmitted diseases and subsequently avoiding oral malignancy. Oral cancer is the only cancer where there is a high risk of disability, the surgical procedures often do not have a good cosmetic outcome. It is a responsibility of the society to avoid any malpractice that acts as an obstacle in the growth of our society.

I am now sharing with you a story of a villager who fought back cancer along with his family at a government hospital in Patna. With great strength he came out of oral cancer and now he is leading a normal life. When he contracted the disease he was unaware of the disease and what impact it would have on his future will be narrated.

STORY OF PAPPU JHA

Pappu Jha, a resident of Khagaria district in Bihar, related his story to me. When I met him, I discovered that he too had gone through tough times in life and life-threatening situations. Meeting him helped me understand the evils of tobacco consumption. As a child, he was born in a village named Dumariya in the Khagaria district. His father was a Pandit who took care of the Mandir in the village. He was called by the people in the village for different ceremonies and pujas. The money and donations given to him provided a decent source of sustenance for his family.

He remembers going to the local village school as a child. He was naughty and was the only boy in the family, followed by three sisters. His mother was a homemaker who was busy doing household duties and raising four naughty children. He says he was never interested in studies. He was busy creating trouble for the teachers, which resulted in him getting reprimanded on an everyday basis. Slowly, his interest dissipated, and he wanted to leave school and enter a work life that was productive and would bring in some money for the family.

He spoke to his father about it. His father wanted him to study ; however, he gathered a lot of news about his school from his teachers. Eventually, Kamlesh Jha decided to give up on Pappu's education and train him practically in reading scriptures and learning the mantras and hymns to begin working as a Pandit in the village. Within a few years, he was trained in all kinds of puja rituals, and households began to get in touch with the family for all kinds of ceremonies in their homes. By now, his sisters were all married off, and he was contributing positively to the household kitty. His father was now middle-aged developed a considerable amount of physical illness, refusing to be monitored by a doctor regularly.

Many families approached his family regarding Pappu 's marriage. His parents were on the lookout for a suitable bride for him. His marriage was fixed by his parents and other members. There were celebrations as everyone was thrilled with the anticipation of getting a new bride in the household. However, the happiness was short-lived when Pappu 's ailing father passed away, and the family was deeply grieved by their loss. The marriage date was postponed for a year's time frame. The marriage was a low-key affair, with all the ceremonies performed by his uncle, who lived in Rourkela and worked as a professor at a college.

The new bride was ambitious and plain-spoken. She settled into the family, looking after her widowed mother-in-law and her sisters- in-law, who were married and lived in nearby villages. Within a few years, he had three children. The eldest was Rajiv, the second son was named Sanjeev, and the third daughter was Naina. Most of Pappu 's friends were leaving the village in search of work. Pappu's wife was now eager to leave the village and move to Delhi for work. She wanted their children to study in good schools and make a decent living. Life for Pappu was not easy as he was not educated enough to even get a job as a peon in a company. Under the pressure of his wife, he took the help of his brother-in-law, who worked in a pharmacy shop in Delhi.

Life in the village was free from dust and pollution, and he did not have to worry about rooms and space for accommodating his family. In Delhi, the cost of living was so high that he had to live with his family in a chawl, which was just a one-room accommodation. One side of the room was converted into a kitchen, while a five-member family lived in whatever space was left. The immediate problem for the family was to raise funds for their daily sustenance. Pappu's brother-in-law told him there was work available in parking lots, where the job was to collect money from people parking their vehicles. The only task was to help them park their vehicles in the right place and keep an eye on the parking area.

The work did not sound tough, and it provided him easy money to sustain his family. Meanwhile, his wife found a job as a laborer in one of the factories in the area. Together, the couple was able to gather enough money to stay in Delhi. The children were enrolled in nearby government schools. Life continued for many years, and Pappu stayed with his family in Delhi. One major thing he began after arriving in Delhi was chewing tobacco and smoking biri, which is made from tobacco leaves.

While telling me this, he looked at me and asked why he was the only one affected by it. All his friends did it, and so many people in the village smoked biri-yet no one else got this disease. Why was he the only one affected ? It must be his previous karma, he said, that caused him to suffer from such a deadly disease.

He had no symptoms of the disease while in Delhi. All those years spent in the chawl, he worked in the parking area. He developed a habit of eating betel leaves, betel nuts, and zarda. When the kids grew up, he decided to go back to the village because he and his wife were not in good health. The eldest child was applying for jobs after completing his studies, and the younger boy had also finished his education. His daughter was old enough to get married.

The eldest one soon got a job in a finance company, and the youngest boy was also locally employed in the village. His daughter got married a few years after returning to the village. One day, he found that the right side of his face had completely swollen. He also found that the gums, teeth, and everything were painful. He thought he probably had a tooth infection and needed to see a dentist.

The dentist was quite surprised to see his bad condition. He gave him medicines and sent him back home. No amount of medicine, good food, or anything else provided the respite he needed. He could hardly chew food, so he was on soft food and milk for a few days. When he found that the local doctor's medicine did not offer relief, he went to Bhagalpur to see a senior doctor. The pain and his condition had worsened.

The doctor requested further investigation by ordering an orthopantomogram. It revealed a growth on the right side of the oral cavity. The doctor was very frank with him and said that his hospital was not equipped to handle his condition. He would need to go to Patna for better treatment. Accompanied with his second son, he went to Patna to see another senior doctor, and after assessing his condition, they said it was crucial for Pappu to undergo surgery at the earliest. They just mentioned that there was a growth in the oral cavity. The cost of the operation was too high, and Pappu did not have the funds. One of the senior doctors then referred him to Mahavir Hospital in Patna.

This is a cancer research institute that treats poor cancer patients for free. After visiting Mahavir Hospital premises, he was taken to a senior oncologist who, after reviewing his condition and consulting his team, decided to operate on him on a specified date. He did not know much about the procedure that followed, but after a few surgeries, it was discovered that he was in the second stage of cancer. In the subsequent surgeries, a part of his right jaw and teeth were removed. He remembered the painful days and said there was a hole in his cheek after the surgery. He was a frightful sight.

He stayed in the hospital for nearly three months, during which he underwent chemotherapy and radiation. I would like to tell my readers that Pappu did not want to remember this part of the story, so he did not go into too much detail. He only provided a rough sketch of his recovery. Before sending him back home, the doctors took him to a plastic surgeon for grafting so that he could live life with minimal cosmetic disfigurement.

This was all the conversation I could have with him because there were two barriers. First, his voice was not clear due to the partial removal of his jaw, and second, he was not interested in the trip down memory lane. Today Pappu lives in the village along with his wife and his second son's family which includes his daughter in law and two grandchildren. He is happy doing puja and taking care of the main temple and its deity. There is an empathetic environment around him which takes care of him and his family. It is my heartfelt prayer to Lord Sai Maharaj to let Pappu live mindfully and lead a healthy life which is happy and healthy. Let no bad habits cross his way and the time spent with his family be blissful and happy.

Now I am going to move to another story and perspective of life which will deal with a bitter truth of life. Not all of us get lucky in life. We all know that everyone suffering from cancer does not go back home. However we all need a respectable end to our journey. In cancer when the case worsens the financial expenses go sky rocketing. Many families look for help from outside to support their sick member of the family. Now I am going to describe such an institution which is full of empathy and love for terminally ill patients who are in the last stage of their illness.

UNDERSTANDING PALLIATIVE CARE

Once the diagnosis of not just cancer but any terminal illness takes place then the existence of the patient is judged more with a clinical snippet which is mentioned in some corner of our medical textbook. Then we stop seeing the person as an individual but more like a case history. There are times when the patients don't have enough money to undergo treatment for terminal illnesses. Most of the time when the case is detected the patient is either extremely old or the case is detected at an advanced stage. The poor geriatric patients are many time sent to elderly care home to have a peaceful, dignified and soulful death. There can be a debate about why one should go for care centers when diagnosed with a terminal illness. We will answer these questions in this chapter.

Medical Ethics

Medical ethics are the moral principles that guide the medical professionals and the fraternity which help in taking care of their patient and public welfare. It is built on four principles:

Autonomy

It is basically the patient's right to accept or refuse a treatment. This principle is where palliative medicine and clinical medicine should go hand in hand while giving the diagnosis the patients comfort and welfare should be kept in mind. Not just financially but also the emotional aspects of the families should be taken into consideration while taking the treatment protocol. Apart from this, patients should be involved actively in their treatment plan by explaining their diagnosis in detail. The patient should be given complete right to decide their course of treatment. The communication process should be extremely transparent. The patient should be allowed to ask questions about their condition. Apart from this the patient should be explained about all the possible treatment options depending on their financial affordability. The patient should be given even enough privacy while deciding the course of the treatment. While undergoing any procedure the patient should be given a proper explanation about the procedure, the outcomes and the risk of undergoing the procedure. The clinician should take a sign of from the patient and the care taker for medico legal cases. in the future.

Non maleficence

Non maleficence means any medical procedure or any part of the medical treatment which is performed with an intention to do no harm to the patient. Under the principle of palliative care the risk benefit ratio while treating a patient is considered of prime importance. The patient's life is considered more important than anything. It also aims at improving the standard of living of the patient with the disease with dignity and greater self respect.

Beneficience

Under the principle of beneficence, doing everything in the benefit of the patient is of prime importance. Under such situations clinician should avoid using the principle of paternalism, rather involve the patient in the treatment process, allow them to be a part of their clinical journey of treatment, keep their trusted family members involved. Clinicians cannot pressurise any of their patients to take treatment which is not agreeable to them. Rather patients should be allowed to decide and make their own decision at their own free will and should undergo their treatment where the clinicians role is that of an advisor for their patients is exceptionally important.

Justice

It is the principle under the medical ethics where one considers the treatment of their patients in such a way that they consider only the process which is right for the patient considering the risk and benefit of the treatment. The fairness about the utilization of resources is of prime importance, righteousness is extremely important under this principle.

Introduction

Palliative medicine is the branch of medicine that deals with the aim of improving the quality of life of the patient and families who are experiencing terminal illness like cancer by not just dealing with the alleviation of the mental effect of the burden of suffering from an advanced stage of terminal illness but also alleviating from the short term symptoms as well which includes pain and other distressing symptoms. For cancer patients it is extremely important to consider this option apart from the allopathic measure.

The need for Palliative Care

It is needed to reduce the stress or distressing features associated with the disease, it provides dignity to the patient while undergoing the journey of the illness. It also provides a balance in the process of the treatment journey by reducing the anxiety associated with the disease by allowing the patient to ask questions and giving them information about the disease, course and treatment in a language which is lucid and easy for the patient and the family members to understand depending on the patient's understanding level. The anxiety and stress associated with death is removed making them realise that death is just an outcome which is not to be scared of. This care can be provided as a multidisciplinary approach.

Provisions of Palliative Care

There can be multiple provisions for providing palliative care. It can be facility based, inpatient, outpatient, home based, bedside and via road side clinic basis. Palliative medicine has become the need of the hour where the patients pain is dealt and counselled with compassion for those patients where curative treatment has more risk than benefits and it is given to help the patient reduce the current symptoms than to cure the disease in general to alleviate the current issue to improve their quality of life.

Palliative Care for Children

When one looks at a geriatric individual with terminal illness or a paediatric patient undergoing the same illness. We find that both are the extreme sides of the spectrum where whether a paediatric or a geriatric individual. If a person develops a disease like cancer then symptoms of the disease are more important. An adult with symptoms can still be counselled but a child is even more challenging. Alleviating their symptoms is of prime importance because at times the clinicians considering their age keep their parents more into confidence than the patient itself underestimating their extent of understanding could even supersede the adults. Sometimes it is better to explain to the child about their condition than to keep them in the dark because a young child has more tenacity and resilience to fight any disease than an adult or a geriatric. The main key ingredient is transparency with them because at the end of the day they would realise it by the body language or the behaviour of the people around them.

Signs and Symptoms

Patients of terminal illness want to lead their life with utmost happiness without any emotional baggage about the outcome of their disease that they carry everywhere at times. The biggest problem in many scenarios is the perspective of the society towards the patient with the disease and often objectifying the person's disease than the person themselves. The process of palliative medicine aims more at alleviating the symptoms as prime importance so that their symptoms don't affect their day to day activities in such a way that they lead a more dignified life. In case the patient who experiences extreme pain they are treated by assessing the pain and medication provided according to the dose suitable to the patient palliative medicine. Similarly in case of other symptoms like cachexia, breathlessness, constipation. Each symptom is treated one by one by keeping the disease out of the picture and treated with care to provide relief. At times improving the standard of living outweighs the freedom of a patient of the disease in terminal illness patient where curative treatment has more risks than benefits.

Palliative Care in Children management

There are times in paediatric cases where the children themselves don't know about the things right for their well being. The parents are eventually the people who decide about their children's treatment plan. Keeping the parents, guardian and family members involved in different aspects of the treatment journey forms the principle of palliative care in adults and children. Maintaining extremely clear and transparent communication and trust with them is extremely important for the situation when a child gets sick as patients are more conscious and worried when a child is involved. Alleviating their worries is of prime importance considering the fact that a child has terminal illness.

Palliative medicine can be taken up as multidisciplinary approach alongside the clinical medical as a prime approach

Conclusion

A patient who is suffering from cancer should be clear that there are times when alternate options like palliative medicine could be a saviour in scenarios where the case is beyond the benefit of being treated by a curative approach. It is the responsibility of the patient to understand the fact that not every patient requires curative treatment. The option of either non-invasive alternative treatment and palliative care should also be presented to these patients. Even when a patient who is undergoing chemotherapy or is in a post operative case can also be sent for counselling.

The patient and their family should be sent for counselling so that they are more focused about the personal journey with the disease than comparing the pain and struggles or emotional baggage of other people which creates support and compassion among the patient and their family members. The patient gets the resilience to fight the disease with this freedom. The economic, emotional needs, ability and multiple factors are considered while considering the best way to offer palliative care. It also creates a ray of hope for all the members of the family to fight the war with the disease because these are trying times. Both the patient and treating clinicians cooperation should go hand in hand in order to reduce the pain which is possible with the palliative approach in case of terminally ill patients.

Now I am going to introduce you all to an institution named Karunashraya which is a palliative care hospice with the head office at Bengaluru. I am going to run you through their organisation and then narrate another story of a patient who found ultimate peace in their care before moving to the realm of ultimate peace.

KARUNASHRAYA

The end of life is a bitter reality, it comes as a surprise, and for a few they know that their end is near, and they wait for the day to arrive when they would leave the world for the heavenly abode. People suffering from end-stage cancer are aware that very soon they will leave the world so they are asked by hospitals and doctors to go home and stay with their family and loved ones in their last days. For a patient and their family it is a tough task, as end-stage cancer is extremely painful. At times people are so weak and frail that they cannot handle their own body weight and need support. Under these circumstances the life of the patient and the families looking after them get caught in a web, and normal functioning of life for other members as well becomes completely impossible. Families and the patient need support to function in a regular manner. There is a need for mental and physical support which is not easily available.

The word Karunashraya is a combination of two words, Karuna and Ashraya. The Hindi word Karuna means compassion, and ashraya is another word for home. A home that is built with compassion for the sick and the ailing who are taking rest in the last stage of life. They are about to cross over into a world which we have no idea about, but it will definitely get them away from the constant pain and sickness with which they are ridden.

Karunashraya is a 300-bedded hospice located in Bangalore that deals in palliative care and looks after people suffering from the last stage of cancer. The inspiration behind this institution is personal to the people who have stood with the thought that people in pain and sickness need to have an exit from this world which is peaceful and full of dignity. Some of the stalwarts who started this initiative are Kishore S. Rao, Dr. Nagesh Simha, Gurmeet Singh Randhawa, and other members of the Karunashraya trust. The hospital is headed by the CEO Matthew George Chandy.

End-Stage Cancer Supported by Karunashraya

Inpatient Pain Management and Comfort:

One of the biggest troubles for cancer patients is pain management especially in case of terminally ill patients. In palliative care the patients get the constant care and attention of doctors and health care providers who help them in combating unbearable pain. They have constant access to medications and therapies which would not be available at home. Karunasharaya also helps patients with home care as well.

Emotional and Socio Psychological Support:

It is a fact that we all have limited breath and one day we all will leave for the eternal abode. Patients who know they have limited time available with them are constantly under fear, anxiety and depression due to their condition. They need a compassionate hearing and hands that hold them with care. The care giving institutions have counselling teams who take care of the emotional well-being of the patients.

Dignity and Respect:

During the last stages of one's life people want to cross over to the unknown with love and dignity. They do not want to be treated like a dead load with no hand in their own decision making. Outsiders tend to make decisions on their behalf which might not be taken in good taste by the patient. A sick person's preferences and routine is compromised which hurts them. At a care home a patient is cared for keeping these small factors in mind.

Companionship and Connection:

Special care is taken by the hospice to take care of the patient's emotional balance. Families are allowed to visit the patients to keep the emotional connection alive in people. This helps in creating lasting memories for patients and families. The hospital understands the value of companionship so that they do not feel isolated from the world. Spirituality becomes extremely important for people dealing with end stage cancer to keep them emotionally and spiritually agile. They help them with spiritual support by listening to religious discourses to get a deeper understanding of life and life after death.

Legacy and Closure:

Care centers help patients with their last wishes like leaving behind messages for loved ones or meeting their friends and relatives for the last time. There are many unfinished matters which people want to close before they leave. The institution supports in finding a closure and resolving issues for the patients so that they leave the world peacefully.

To get a better understanding about the functioning of the institution I decided to collect a case study for the benefit of my readers. I initially spoke to Sham Gopal Krishnan who works for the institution and looks after the communication function of the organisation. I was later introduced to Michelle who heads the psycho counselling division. She gave me a story which I will relate to you in the next chapter of the book.

THE STORY OF PETER GEORGE AT KARUNASHRAYA

When I spoke to Michelle at Karunasharay she gave me the story of Peter George. Peter was born in Bangalore to a young couple. They had two sons. Oliver the eldest one was around 10 years older to Peter. The house was not that blissful as there were constant fights and disagreements between husband and wife. This finally ended on a sad note when the couple decided to get divorced. It was decided that the elder son who was around 12 years would stay with the father and the younger son who was just around 2 years moved to Chennai with his mother. Mother started to work with a convent in Chennai. When the younger son was around 7 years old the mother died and the younger son, Peter became an orphan. The convent could not connect to any relative of Peter so he was moved to the orphanage run by the convent.

Peter grew up well. He completed his education and started on his own by putting up his own business. His business grew and his major business connections were in Africa. As time lapsed he met a girl of his choice and he decided to get married. Very soon Peter and his wife were blessed with a baby girl. One day in Bangalore he met a distant relative who knew his parents. He told him that he was too small when his parents got divorced. During the process of the divorce his parents had decided that his elder brother would stay with his father and he would move to Chennai with his mother. This filled Peter's heart with great joy and he sought his brother's phone number and called him. Ever since the brothers remained in touch and wished each other on Christmas and Birthdays.

Peter's little abode of happiness was happy and full of smiles till his business got affected and things started going downhill. His business in Africa had started giving him trouble due to which there were frequent disagreements and fights at home. As the crisis deepened the fights started getting more serious and difficult to handle. It is at this point of time Peter's wife decided to move away from him to another place along with their daughter. Peter was now in an estranged relationship in which his wife and his daughter rarely got in touch with him. Slowly Peter's health started deteriorating and when he met the doctors he was diagnosed with Cancer. The difficulty level deepened around the covid period in which Peter's health started deteriorating and the cancer had spread to the bone. He was in the last stage of Cancer and he was all on his own taking care of himself. He just had two close friends who lived close by who used to take care of his fooding and checked on him everyday. With the passing of time Peter was unable to take care of himself and he was also getting old. He was 67 and was unable to take care of his basic needs.

It was at this time that he got to know about Karunasharaya, where people were taken care of in their last stage of cancer. So he looked for the number of Karunasharaya and he called up the hospice for help. He got to speak to Micehlle and he told her that he was in Chennai and needed to move to Bangalore as his health was in a bad condition due to which he was not able to take care of himself. Peter was a great believer of God and he felt that one way or the other god would cure him and save his life. So even in his bad condition he wanted to try some other kind of medication which would help him get better. As a hospice Karunasharaya does not allow patients to take medication from some other hospital and stay at their care center. This was in the year 2021 and Covid was still raging. The fear that other frail patients might take up some or the other kind of infection was worrisome for the caregivers. So Michelle asked him to arrange for his own accommodation and take home care services from the hospice. So Peter called up his brother and sought his help. The elder brother was more than willing to accommodate him at his home and help him through this difficult patch.

Peter was now able to try other kinds of treatments possible for cancer. The hospice did not discourage other kinds of medication. He was just asked to come to the hospital and get himself checked by the doctor and he got the attention of the home care team as well. Slowly his health started deteriorating and he had to make an incremental effort to even go to the bathroom. Taking care of him was becoming difficult for the elderly couple. The information regarding Peter's deteriorating health condition was shared by the home care team to the hospice therefore Peter's family was advised to move him to the hospice so that they can go ahead and take care of themselves. Peter had now come to terms with the fact that his end was near and it was only advisable for him to go to the hospice.

After Peter moved to the hospice Michelle and team took care of his mental well being and pain management was taken by the palliative team of doctors at the hospital. It was there that he learnt that there were many kinds of programs which were held on an everyday basis for the patients like songs and dances to entertain people and take their mind off their current condition. Participating in these events brought a thrill in the face of the sick and ailing.

There were other activities which were undertaken by the team like regular meetings with family members, friends and relatives to build lasting memories for all. It was just days before his death that Michelle asked if he wanted to meet his wife and daughter. Peter with the passage of time had come to terms with his condition and thought about his marriage as a thing of distant past. He was satisfied and did not want to upset his condition any more. He told Michelle he was happy and satisfied. He said he had not been in touch with them for years so he did not want to disturb them. Peter smiled and talked till his last days of survival and one day in the morning he left for the heavenly abode. There was peace on his face and the pain which had disturbed had become silent. The team at the hospice handed over the body to the family members and he was later cremated to achieve eternal peace. I pray to Lord Sai Ram for the eternal peace of Peter and all those who have taken shelter at the Karunashraya hospice in different parts of India.

THE HEALING POWER OF MEDITATION AND MINDFULNESS IN CANCER RECOVERY

People who have written about cancer have poured their hearts out while narrating their stories. This book would not be complete if I did not mention my journey post-chemotherapy. This is where all the physical agony and pain started. I want my readers to know this part of the story, as it is a critical part of the recovery process.

Once I was through all the surgeries, my doctor, Dr. Shashikant Mishra, asked me to take the chemotherapy session, which is an important part of the medication. I had heard many sordid stories about pain post-chemo, and mentally, I was not ready to go through it. Dr. Mishra was very candid in his approach and said the treatment would not be over without chemo. Unwillingly, I agreed to it. I had absolutely no choice. My husband, Aditya, and Dr. Mishra were both on the same side. The doctor, with his most charming behavior, convinced me that it is the application of medicine on the affected spot.

When I went for the first session, I found that the process was rather simple, not anticipating the effect of the session later. As I reached home, it seemed as if my insides were on fire, and there was an irritation in the bladder that was beyond imagination. Slowly, I was developing a fever that was far beyond my contemplation. I did not know what to do. The pain and the irritation were too much to bear. I had two pairs of innocent eyes watching me from a distance. My eldest daughter was 11, and the youngest was 4, all at a loss for words, seeing me in so much pain. We called Dr. Mishra and updated him about my state of affairs. He had given me medicines that I had to take for nearly two days until the pain and fever lasted. I was in no condition to take care of my family. My husband administered food and medicine to me while I lay combating the pain.

This went on for eight weeks, and with each chemotherapy session, my condition became worse. My eyes were bloodshot red for a few weeks, and visibility was low. I could hardly manage due to the consistent pain in my bladder. As per my medical condition, my bladder had grown smaller during the treatment process, so I had to urinate very frequently, which was extremely embarrassing. I could hardly hold on to my urine.

Eight weeks lapsed, and as time went by, I had no idea how long it would take to emerge from pain and anguish. The maximum I walked was on my way to the bathroom. The pain intensified at times, and I could see no light at the end of the tunnel. I would cry myself to sleep occasionally, as I could not imagine being in such a miserable condition for the rest of my life. I was a corporate trainer before coming to Anand, but I had become a pitiful subject of discussion among people in the colony.

I visited the hospital many times, reeling in pain. I asked Dr. Mishra to help me and prescribe medication to combat the pain. I could see the helplessness in his eyes as he witnessed my agony. He would conduct tests to check my condition and ask me to sit in a tub full of water to counter the burning sensation. Later, he would send me home to rest. Due to the water treatment, the pain would temporarily subside, only to resurface when I returned home. However, one thing I would like to mention is that my doctor understood my pain, and he was not immune to it. I could see the pain in his eyes whenever I went to him. My mother came to see me a few weeks later and saw me reeling in pain. I do not have words of praise for her. The composure she maintained after seeing me in such grotesque pain showed her resilience and resolute behavior.

The first thing she observed was that I was not eating enough. My diet had completely collapsed, and I did not have enough strength to fight against the pain I was experiencing. The entire house, my husband, and children were all in utter chaos. With her coming home, she took charge of the house, employed new maids, and set me on a routine of having meals. The biggest discovery we made on the first day my mom came over was that I had difficulty swallowing hard food. For a long time, I had been on semi-solid and liquid food, which caused difficulty in swallowing.

With time the severity of the pain had started to diminish, but every time I went to the bathroom, I endured a terrible experience while passing urine. The pain in my bladder persisted. It had been nearly six months, and the pain still lingered. Life was limping back to normal, but I could do nothing about the pain while urinating. I had started thinking that perhaps I would have to live with this pain for the rest of my life. I began taking small walks outside my house, trying to get some fresh air. One day, during my walk, a lady came up and introduced herself as Sujata Padhee.

She lived in the lane across from my house. I never got the chance to introduce myself to the new community I was part of. She invited me to her place for a Reiki session. I had never heard of Reiki in my life. Sujata explained it to me as a meditation session that would help me in my recovery process. I thought there was no harm in trying it once. When I entered the house, it was filled with ladies who were holding each other's hands, and the prayer was about to start. There was a rather stout Gujarati lady named Ami Shah, who was the master Reiki practitioner. She asked me to close my eyes and feel the energy flowing through the group. Music started to play, and the Reiki master began to speak in a soothing tone as we all closed our eyes.

I sat in my chair, silent, and within a matter of seconds, I felt warmth flowing through my body. In my mind's eye, I sensed a calmness I had not felt in a long time. I was uncertain if I was awake or asleep. However, I could hear a calm voice asking us all to be mindfully aware of the energy flowing through our bodies, from our head to our toe. This must have lasted for around 15 minutes, and afterward, everyone rubbed their hands to transfer the heat of their palms to their faces and eyes. Later, the hostess,

Sujata, served us snacks, which I ate while chatting with the other women in the group. After some time, I realized that I had not thought about visiting the bathroom for the past hour or more. I immediately realized that, by God's grace, I had stumbled upon a gold mine. I approached the master and asked her what the course was about, as I wanted to learn her meditation technique. She did not live too far from my house. I scheduled a time to be with her and learn the first stage of Reiki. I learned the first stage of Reiki and practiced it for a month. The pain I felt during urination increased in the beginning and subsequently had begun to recede.

Slowly and steadily with each passing day the pain was ebbing off.Mindfully I practiced and within a month I was ready for doing the second session of Reiki which was used for distant healing. My self confidence had sky rocketed and now I was ready to face the world. I wanted to tell the medical fraternity how I had come out of the deadly pain which I was going through. It was a Eureka moment for me. So I went to Muljibhai along with my husband. Dr. Mishra and other doctors who had seen me in a deteriorated condition were extremely happy to see me back in proper health smiling and talking about my health.

One of the doctors in the room said he had heard about energy healing, but never had come across people who actually recovered with the help of this. I was so glad to hear it. So, the medical fraternity is aware of its existence. The lady who trained me in Reiki told me that Reiki was extremely effective when people have gone thtough through chemo sessions. It helps them battle the pain and the side effects of chemo.

It has been 13 years now, and I tried to push all these incidents out of my memory lane into a forgotten corner of my brain. A few years ago, I started writing a book on cancer survivors, when I spoke to Dr. Maheash Desai again. I asked him if he had taken any meditation courses to forget the pain of cancer treatment. He shared his own story and mentioned going to a mindfulness course and meditation sessions conducted by Deepti Ghatge in Pune. She used to be a filmmaker and worked as a writer.director, producer who took up meditation many years ago and now runs mindfulness and meditation courses in Pune professionally. This is a very interesting piece of conversation that I want my readers to know, read, and understand the effect of meditation on all kinds of physical and mental stress we undergo in everyday life. I have discussed one kind of meditation in my story. Let me give you the details of the other kind of meditation as described by mindfulness trainer and teacher Deepti Ghatge.

Rendezvous with Deepti Ghatge

Deepti, you run mindfulness and meditation courses online and in person. How did your journey with meditation start?

My journey with meditation started in the year 2000. I meditated for the first time, and it was a wonderful experience. I was in college at the time. Since the year 2012, I have started meditating on an everyday basis. In the years 2015, 2016, and 2017, I faced adverse health challenges. Looking back I feel as though it was something that happened for the best as it completely changed my priorities and perspective on life and changed the path of my life.

How did you start with your setup in Pune?

Even though I loved filmmaking, I felt that a goal-oriented life was no longer my calling. It took time for me to leave my passion as I loved artistic films and had invested several years in it. However, I realised that going forward I wanted to dedicate my time to mindfulness and meditation.

How would you explain mindfulness?

Mindfulness is the awareness that emerges when we pay attention on purpose, in the present moment, and non-judgementally to things as they are.

Is it living beyond your joy or your state of despair?

No, I would not put it that way; it is living in the present moment, being fully aware of whatever one is experiencing in the present moment. When one brings full awareness to what is, the present moment gets transformed. It is a beautiful and richer way of living.

How does mindfulness help?

Mindfulness radically changes the way we live our life. By bringing awareness in our everyday waking moments we transform them, create a pause and reduce reactivity. This translates into better decision making, less stress, better health, increased ability to cope with challenges, better memory and focus, reduced anxiety etc. We start becoming aware of our body, emotions, thoughts, impulses and this awareness creates a richer life which helps us to go beyond pain and pleasure and experience a state of joy and peace which is not dictated by outer circumstances.

Whom do you enroll for the mindfulness courses that you run?

I run multiple modules for meditation and mindfulness sessions. People enrolling in the courses are from all over the world from different cultures as well ethnicities. They include executives, CEOs, chairpersons of multinational companies, bankers, pharma companies, renowned doctors, professionals in healthcare, education, women taking care of children, and the community at large. We are also working with the police force in Pune. We work with those undergoing specific health challenges. Our mindfulness courses are charged but we do not accept any fees for any of our meditation sessions.

What is the name of the institute and from where did you learn mindfulness?

We run under the umbrella "A Mindful Breath". The mindfulness course is developed by Oxford University and Oxford Mindfulness Foundation. I am a certified trainer and teacher from them. It is a highly researched, scientific and evidence based programme. It is based on the latest research in psychology and it has taken some Eastern traditions as well. It is a unique course. The meditations that we do are of different types and several of them are my own.

Have your participants given you the feedback that your course is a wonderful experience?

Almost everyone who has completed the course has given us this feedback. They have appreciated the course and the journey which comes along with it. They have found some tools to cope with things and to live life in a more fulfilling way. However, there have been a few people who have felt that this is not for them which we completely understand and respect. Meditation and mindfulness are not the only ways by which people can overcome something.

Do people with terminally ill disease, specifically cancer, come for courses offered by your organisation?

We have not had any terminally ill patients with us yet. However, we are open to working with them and feel that mindfulness can lead towards a better acceptance and way of life for them.

Sometimes people come looking for a quick fix. But meditation and mindfulness are not a quick fix. They are a way of life. By being in tune with your experience something gets transformed and one is able to live better.

I could not agree more as I went through the same thing which I experienced while going through Reiki. What is the duration of your course?

It is an eight week course, once a week for two hours. The rest of the week people are recommended that they practice what has been taught to them. It is an experiential course, skills training. It is recommended that one does not do this course when they are in the middle of a life changing situation such the demise of a loved one or when one is going through chemo. It would be better if they do it a little after or perhaps before any of these situations arise so that they can have the capacity to build the skills that we teach which will serve them well when they are undergoing challenging life situations.

In a few words can you describe for my readers why living mindfully is necessary?

Meditation and mindfulness is for all of us. Specifically for people who are chronically ill or are suffering they will feel the need to get away from the pain. Mindfulness teaches us to fully be with this challenging moment, and also to learn to look at pain and in many cases transform pain. The studies done by Jon Kabat-Zinn on patients experiencing pain have shown that their pain levels were reduced to as low as 2 on a scale of 0 to 10, 10 being the highest and this was without taking any medication by simply doing the practices.

Meditation brings peace and joy in one's life and amongst other things it brings in a certain "Sehajata" which is an easier, uncomplicated way of being and living and "Svikriti" which is radically accepting the present moment and situation as it is.

Dear Deepti, it was wonderful talking to you. Due to my own acceptance of pain and revival I understand your love for meditation and the mindfulness course that you run. I will pray to **Lord Sai Ram Maharaj** to bless you and your healing abode with health and happiness.

With this I end my journey with survivor stories of cancer. I hope all those who need the strength to fight the disease might gain insight to fight with strength and overpower the pain with force and tenacity. May the blessings of the almighty Sri Sai Maharaj be with you and your family.